A Flat-pack in Greece

A Flat-pack in Greece

Eva Goldsworthy

ISBN: 0 86243 856 X

cover: Y Lolfa

Dinas is an imprint of Y Lolfa

Printed and published in Wales
by Y Lolfa Cyf., Talybont, Ceredigion SA24 5AP
e-mail ylolfa@ylolfa.com
website www.ylolfa.com
tel. (01970) 832304
fax (01970) 832782

Introduction

WHY GREECE? Nearing retirement, one begins to think of returning to one's roots. My roots were in Wales, God's own country, land of purple hills and beautiful people, land of male voice choirs and chapel hypocrites, land of hiraeth (longing). I loved it in all its manifestations, good and bad, but there was just one snag - the weather. Except for a few months in the summer, it either rained or snowed. I had watched new born lambs struggling from the womb on to a wet snowy field, and seen the look of horror on their faces as their feet tentatively tested the slush; however, lambs are tough and they soon recover, or at least are able to make the best of it. But my resilient days were over. At sixty years of age, one needs a little coddling, and I decided to take my creaking bones to a warmer country, planning to live there for the better part of the year, while still keeping a foothold in *hen wlad fy nhadau* (the land of my fathers).

But, again, I hear you ask, "WHY GREECE? Why choose that particular warm country out of all the other possibilities?

Twenty-five years ago, I escaped to Greece from a failed marriage, hoping to sooth the pain by visiting the ancient sites of Delphi, the Parthenon, Epidavros and so on, sites I'd read about as a child. I did, indeed, do this, but early on in the visit, I met and fell in love with a Greek sailor. I was on the rebound, I suppose. He came from the Peloponnese, and he went with me on a trip from Patras to Delphi, crossing the narrow gulf by ferry in the company of a group of gypsies. I fed their monkey with grapes. At Delphi, I touched the stone

that the ancients called the *omphalos*, the navel, or centre, of the
world; and then, the sailor and I held hands and looked down
the great gorge to the sea far below and breathed in that
miraculous air, heavy with thyme and the weight of history,
and I felt a bliss so intense that it ached. I'm afraid my love for
the swarthy sailor lasted for less than a year, but the deeper
love, a deeper wonder, remained, and it was for Greece. This
stayed throughout the subsequent decades, so when the time
came to make a choice, there was no doubt about the country
I would pick to warm my aching limbs. Alas for that poor
sailor: poor Costas, Costas Leopodis, Costas Lionfoot. Would I
have had a litter of cubs by now, had we not parted?

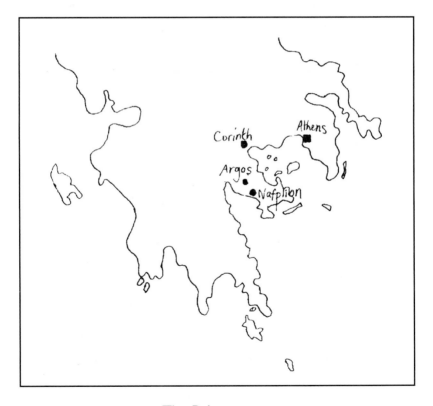

The Peloponnese

Chapter 1

Preparing to Go

I am averse to using lending libraries. Any books I read I want to possess, not just borrow, and this idiosyncrasy also applies to houses. I dislike anything as temporary as renting, so, consequently, I wanted to own my house in Greece, and I began to prepare myself for a venture into the Greek property market. Having heard horror stories of naive foreigners being fleeced by wily Greeks, I realised that, in order to have even partial control over the proceedings, I would have to come to grips with the language. True, I had learned some Greek phrases with Costas, but only of the intimate variety; now, I needed more useful words, sufficient to ask for prices, or check bylaws, or, more mundanely, to read road signs. I had noticed that Greek motorists were very volatile, and I didn't want to go the wrong way down a one-way street. To overcome this communication gap, I enrolled in the City Literary Institute in Holborn, known universally as the City Lit. It is a sprawling, brick building, not far from Holborn tube station and at the end of a narrow alley, next to an Arabian publishing house. Thank goodness, Greek Cyrillic script is a little easier to master than the Arabic variety.

The City Lit. caters for adults and offers a variety of

subjects, one among them being the Greek language. I noticed that many of the day-time students were elderly eccentrics: women dressed in drooping, hand knitted cardigans and masculine boots, and bearded men, mouthing incomprehensible words from incomprehensible books. There were also students of esoteric subjects such as ancient Coptic, and, at the other end of the scale, bewildered foreigners learning basic English. In the canteen I found a mixture of those who surreptitiously ate their own sandwiches, and others who wolfed down hot sausages or shepherds pie, but all of us were engaged in the process of drinking large mugs of tea. The canteen tea was excellent and I guessed that some people wandered in just to drink the best and cheapest 'cuppa' in London.

The old building was a maze of classrooms, and as I made my way to the First Year Greek class, I felt a little guilty. Surely, I should be brushing up my rusty Welsh language (*Yr Iaith Gymraeg*), rather than flirting with an alien tongue. However, I reasoned that Greek is not an alien tongue; some of the most important words in English come directly from the Greek.

> *The hysterical philosopher had colossal therapy to relieve his psychosomatic gastritis.*

There is not a word here that has not had its origins in Greece.

The tutor was a rather heavy Athenian of indeterminate age but already developing the generous stomach sported by most middle-aged Greek men. In England we call it a beer gut, but I didn't know the equivalent expression in Greek, and, in any case, the pregnant protuberance was surely more to do with good food and wine than beer. My class took place in the afternoon, and so the students were either young and unemployed, or old and retired. Mr. Thalassos tried his best to cope with this mixture and, indeed, succeeded in coaxing us, after a few lessons, to read out a short sentence written in Greek script. We didn't understand what it meant, but at least we were able to convert the weird alphabet into sounds.

Gradually, we learnt that *ochi* means no, and *nai* means yes; that *efcharisto* means thank you, and *para-kalo* means please. So, the backpackers among us could ask for food, say thank you for a lift, and deal with any sexual overtures in whichever way they wanted them to go.

My plan was to spend the late spring and summer in Wales, and the autumn and winter in Greece. It seemed an ideal set-up: sunshine throughout the year. However, this was my first mistake. I failed to realise that the god Helios does not always shine. Cold winds from Siberia can cut across to the Mediterranean, freezing the Sahara nights and chilling the seas and the golden beaches. But more of that later.

In tandem with my Greek classes, I began to prepare myself to live cheek by jowl with the average Greek of the twenty-first century, by re-reading Homer's Iliad. That 2,500 year epic (the date is disputed) describes how the Greeks sailed to Troy, to wrest their compatriot, Helen, from the arms of her seducer. Before you scoff at this method of getting to know the Greek psyche, just reflect that a couple of thousand years or so is not long in the chronicle of world history; a mere blink of an eyelid, when compared with the era of Tyrannosaurus Rex. For me, Achilles sulking in his tent, jealous of Agamemnon and his share of the disposal of captured Trojan women, showed the typical attitude of the predatory Greek male, and, in my experience, it had not changed. Then, Helen whose beauty 'launched a thousand ships' and who used it to flirt with the young Trojan prince Paris and elope with him, thus provoking a war between the two nations, was, perhaps, giving an indication of the manipulative tactics of young Greek women, even today. And, what about the gung-ho stance of Helen's husband Menelaus? To get her back, he went about, stirring up the city states to war, a war which had as much justification as our recent invasion of Iraq. To me, human nature doesn't change, and it was apparent that the Ancient Greeks were basically just like any modern Athenian Greek, who climbs up from the Metro in Athens and crosses Omonia Square to buy a newspaper and a small black coffee.

What did I think about Homer's description of homosexuality? To be honest, I was not sure whether to take this on board or not. There was the description of Achilles and his beloved Patroklas; and I remembered that there were soldier-lovers defending the pass at Thermopylae. Was this tendency still prevalent in modern Greece, and, in any case, was it any business of mine? Local customs still seemed to encourage it. Men marry late and insist that their wives are virgins, and the result is that there are too few willing females to go round. How else are young men able to expend their burgeoning testosterone? Thinking back to Costas, I assumed that, when I met him, he had passed through the homo-erotic stage, but the subject never cropped up, and he didn't let on.

Having begun to deal with the language, and consider the problem of Greek mores, the next decision was where to live in this fabulous country. Certainly not Athens. When I remembered that earlier journey, I remembered indifferent food, coagulating chips, bouzouki accompaniment *ad nauseam*, and ritual plate smashing at the end of each meal. No wonder I had flown into the arms of a Greek sailor who looked as if he hailed far from the tavernas in Kolonaki. My choice of location had to be as far away from Athens and the tourist rat-run as possible. Now, Greece is made up of two main sections; the largest includes Athens and the ranges of the Pindus and Olympian mountains, while in the south-west is the Peloponnese, which has been transformed by the Corinth Canal from an isthmus into an island, and holds the towns of Sparta and Patras.

Then, among an assorted group of islands, there is the large island of Crete. At that time, there were no direct flights there, and Athens airport was a dreary place in which to hang around, so I discounted Crete as a possible home in which to settle. Also, I remembered WWII stories of how the Cretan women on the Omalos plateau had attacked the German parachutists with pitchforks and delayed Hitler's invasion of Russia. If you don't believe this, go to the history books. Maybe, those ferocious peasants still hankered after fighting off an invader, even one as mild as an elderly female writer like myself. So, no thank you to Crete. On the other hand, the Peloponnese (the island of Pelops) had a different sort of history and was equally far away from the bright lights of Athens. True, some say that Mr. Pelops served his son up in a dish, to propitiate the gods; others maintain that the old man was the lover of the sea-king Poseidon, but I felt that these crimes had been expiated by time. Moreover, the island was advertised as beautiful and untouched, and I could vouch for this from my experience with Costas, so, taking all the factors into account, I decided that I would look for my dream house on the Peloponnese.

Not being on the internet, I tramped London, looking for a Greek estate agent. Most Greeks who live in the capital can be found in Camden or King's Cross, or in West Kensington's Queensway. The Camden or King's Cross ones are usually Greek Cypriots, and these estate agents would be specialising in places like Paphos or Limasol, on the island of Cyprus. My best bet was to go to Queensway, for this was where many mainland Greeks had congregated, lured by the attraction of the Orthodox Church in nearby Moscow Road and the Greek Embassy in Holland Park.

Coming out of the Bayswater tube station at the beginning of Queensway, one brushes against Europeans of every variety, interspersed with Muslims and Hindus, and the occasional Aussie venturing abroad from his ghetto in the Earls Court Road, but, in the surrounding shops and houses, there is a preponderance of Greeks. I walked past Greek restaurants emitting delicious smells; I listened to passers-by speaking with what I fondly imagined to be Greek; and in the boutiques and food shops, there were notices in English and Greek. But this was cosmopolitan London, and the Greeks didn't have it all their own way. Halfway down Queensway was Whiteley's emporium, looking like an offshoot of Wembley Stadium, and opposite was an unlikely restaurant-cum-artist's studio, where, for the price of a coffee and a brioche, the customer could sit all morning, sketching a live nude, who was draped across a velvet couch. It was all very exotic, but as to my present concern, I could find no estate agent of any nationality, let alone Greek. Then, on a corner where Queensway meets Bishop's Bridge Road, and within spitting distance of Paddington Station, I saw what I was looking for.

Manolis and Son. Property Developer. Britain and Overseas

Underneath this was a version of the foregoing, written in what I had been taught by Mr. Thalassos to recognise as Greek script.

I pushed open the door and went up a staircase to the reception area. The furniture gleamed with lavender polish, and on the walls there were posters of idyllic beaches; not all were of the travel brochure type. Many posters illustrated Byzantine heroes. The Greeks are not as crazy about pre-Christian classical remains as we are, but prefer to reproduce the frescoes and wall paintings that date from the later

Byzantine era. One poster caught my eye, and I read the English caption.

The Raising of Lazarus.
Church of the Pantanassa. Mistra. 1428.

It was a coloured reproduction of a bizarre scene. A body, swathed in bandages, was being hauled up with ropes by workmen, who were turning their heads away and puking at the stench. I thought it a bit strong and hurriedly turned to a bland photograph of the Acropolis at sunset.

"Can I help you?" asked Mr. Manolis.

He was a typical middle-class Greek; he had olive skin, impeccable Armani suit, heavy gold rings and, when he spoke, a hint of a gold tooth.

"I -er- I'm thinking of buying a house in Greece," I said.

"Splendid." He looked me up and down.

I'd had experience of Greek predators, before Costas rescued me, but there didn't seem to be any sex in Mr. Manolis' look. It was more a shrewd assessment of my financial situation. He narrowed his eyes and put his fingers together, making a steeple, and said slowly,

"For yourself?"

"Yes."

He took a brochure out of his desk and handed it to me. His hands were podgy white against the gold rings. The brochure was heavy and expensively produced, and showed a villa with a swimming pool in the foreground, a smattering of olive trees, and the obligatory young woman in full traditional dress. Did she come with the house, I was tempted to ask, but I resisted because I didn't think Mr. Manolis showed any sign of a sense of humour.

"Will you recruit locally, or will you bring your own staff?" he asked.

He was either short-sighted, or he had completely miss-read

my outfit. I was wearing an antique dress that I had bought off a second-hand stall in the Portobello Road, and for an added touch, I had put on high-heeled shoes. Mr. Manolis looked about sixty. Perhaps I reminded him of high fashion when he was on the loose, in his younger days.

"It would be wise to get a local man to maintain the swimming pool," he continued, as he reluctantly tore his eyes away from my satin cleavage.

Obviously, I had miss-read him, too! I rose with dignity, gave him back the brochure and said that I would put some thought to the matter. We shook hands, and I felt his clammy touch all the way back to Hackney. My friends in Graham Road were appalled.

"Typical macho," they said. "You'll get nowhere with these London Greeks. You must go to the actual place. You'll get a better idea on the spot and you will be able to experience the ambience."

I liked the word ambience. It reminded me of another word: environ. I had first come across them in a tattered *Blue Guide to Greece*, but my well thumbed copy was becoming useless. The print was too small to read, with or without glasses. Of course, my friends were right. I had to go and test the waters, the clear blue waters of the Mediterranean, where multi-coloured fish swim in a translucent sea. I booked a cheap week-end return on a British Airways flight to Athens.

Chapter 2

Getting There

Unlike that first journey to Greece, when I fled from an unsatisfactory marriage, I was now quite blasé about air travel. In the intervening years, I had flown several times to Africa, and had often holidayed in France and Spain. I had even flown up to Scotland from Stanstead Airport! But as we crossed the Alps and into Italy, the old excitement came back. There was a map in the net pocket of the seat in front of me, and I smoothed it out to where it showed the Peloponnese, looking for a sign that would guide me to the ideal spot for a house. Greece's Peloponnese is shaped like a hand clawing down to Africa, but with the little finger missing. Between the thumb and the index is a wide bay, and I could just make out the name, written in thin spidery letters.

The Argonic Gulf

Argonic, from Argos! Where Agamemnon set off for the Trojan war! I quickly found the town of Argos on the little map, but it was several miles inland. He couldn't have set out from there. The fleet must have set sail from a nearby port. I traced down the map with my finger and came to the obvious place, a town on the edge of the gulf. Eureka! Squinting at the small lettering, I made out the name Nauplion. I mouthed the word slowly, lingering on the syllables, Naf-pli-on.

(Mr.Thalassos: In Greek, the letter U is pronounced F)

I had found my base of operation, a town with its feet in the sea, blue hills in the background, and probably topped by a Byzantine church. I decided to go there right away, as soon as we arrived in Greece.

"Fasten seat belts, please," said the Captain. "We will be landing at Athens airport in twenty minutes. The weather is fine and sunny with a slight, fresh wind."

I folded up the map as the plane began its descent through small patches of cloud. Gradually, the blur below began to separate into roads and trees and houses, and, to my surprise, this entrance into reality set me in a panic. What was I letting myself in for? A single, middle-aged woman with an impractical dream, I had just three days to get to this place called Nafplion, find a hotel and an estate agent, and view some property, and all with less than a dozen words of the language.

"Don't worry," said my friends in Dalston, "everyone speaks English, everywhere."

And what happens if they don't? For example, what's the Greek for Estate Agent?

The plane lurched to a halt and I emerged from the cabin into the warm Greek air. It was 6am Greenwich Mean Time, 5am Greek time, and the airport was almost deserted. My companions on the journey had been package tourists. They were soon whisked off in a couple of Thompson's coaches, and I was left alone, apart from the immigration clerk, and two Austrian students who were sleeping on benches. When the clerk returned my passport, I asked him how I could get to Nafplion. He barely looked up, just jerked his head to the road outside and returned to his paperback. Hardly a warm welcome; not much of a "Come to sunny Greece" there! One of the Austrian students stirred and muttered in his sleep; the clerk turned over a page of his book; and the airport looked like settling back into its previous torpor. Then, another British plane arrived and there was a momentary bustle. This time, the Thompson coach was late, and the passengers hung around, shivering in summer clothes. The second Austrian turned over, irritable at being disturbed. Eventually, the bus arrived, with an English tour-guide. He'd obviously been having trouble and was in no mood to help an elderly female who was not one of his party.

"Nafplion? Dunno. Ask the passport clerk."

The coach left and I went outside, with a vague idea of hitching a lift, but then I understood what the clerk had meant when he jerked his head towards the concourse. There, on the tarmac, were ranged a dozen empty buses, each with its own number and destination in a window above the driver's cab, and one, of course, must be indicating Nafplion. But which one? None of the hieroglyphics measured up to my memory of the word that I had found on the map. The wind blew straight off the sea, from Glifada, and I wrapped my anorak more tightly round my body. Thank goodness I had included it in my luggage. I looked at my watch. An hour had gone by and I was losing precious time out of the brief weekend. When would the inert row of buses come to life? Was there some Greek trade union that prevented any movement before 6am? Then, the bus drivers began to arrive; cheerful, middle-aged men, carrying their lunch boxes and cracking jokes.

"*Yassou, Giorgio, pos pragmata?*" (How are things?)

I went up to one of them and asked tentatively,

"Nafplion?"

He answered in voluble Greek and, when I shook my head hopelessly, he led me to one of the buses. The sign on the front didn't look anything like Nafplion, but what could I do? I climbed up the step, put some small change in the ticket machine, and sat down. Initially, there were few passengers, but as the bus moved on towards Athens, it filled up until there was only standing room. Were we going to be squashed like this all the way to Nafplion?

The airport is two miles out of Athens and, as we got nearer, I could see the Acropolis through the trees and, at its summit, the Parthenon, that temple to the city's goddess, Pallas Athene. The passengers carried on chatting among themselves, some men reading *Ta Nea* (the daily newspaper), and a group of school children swapped Pokemon cards. Couldn't they see the incredible sight framing the bus windows? Familiarity, I supposed. After all, perhaps I would be the same, if I were fortunate enough to live at the foot of Snowdon. Greece has to function as a modern state, but it is superimposed over an ancient past, and this gives a curious juxtaposition of the old with the new. As the bus entered Athens and Vouliagmenis Street, a lighting shop, with all manner of chandeliers and shades, which would have fitted well into John Lewis' Stores in Oxford Street, was here set next to Hadrian's Arch, that edifice erected by the Roman Emperor early in the second century as a P.R. job to butter up the Greek senators. Rome always had an inferiority complex about the Greeks because, even though they had conquered them, they were in awe of their intellect. The bus continued, and while some passengers got off, others took their places. It drove through the heart of Athens, past the elegant King George Hotel, past the public gardens heavy with flowering trees, past the paths, dotted with cypresses, that lead up to the Acropolis. Then, the atmosphere began to change. The bus left behind the posh shops and the cypress groves and entered into an area which reminded me of a murky day at Cardiff Docks, or the steel town of Port Talbot. The appearance of the passengers changed also. Neat suits and coiffed hair gave way to something rougher and more peasant-like, and, for the first time that morning, I felt that I was in a foreign country instead of a Hollywood film set. Factories emitted gritty smoke, the smuts floating inside the bus; crooked houses were squashed together, leaning against the grimy factory walls, relics of a less industrialised period; enormous hoardings, advertising Marlborough Cigarettes or Sony TV's, blotted out whatever ray of sun managed to pierce the fug. The traffic was horrific; cars and lorries and trucks vied with each other for space to move forward, all honking furiously. I was looking forward to getting out of this mêlée and reaching the open road, but at a three-way junction, the traffic became worse and the bus, unbelievably, ploughed across the oncoming flow and careered into an abyss. It was, in fact, a vast hangar full of buses. Fixed to the rafters was a notice in English and Greek.

LEOFORIA PELOPONNESOS
Peloponnese Bus Station

The journey hadn't even begun! Dazed, I got out of the bus and stood in the semi-darkness. The bus driver and the rest of the passengers had gone, but another driver, seeing my bewilderment, pointed to the far end of the hanger, which opened out into daylight and was bustling with activity. I didn't catch on immediately, and he rubbed his thumb and forefinger together with the universal gesture for money.

"*Eee-see-teerio, tickuts,*" he said.

Of course, the booking hall! I had already realised that the few coins I had put in the machine at the airport were not enough to see me through to Nafplion, and I had to buy a proper ticket. I made my way through the gloom to the lighted area. The booking hall was well swept and airy, and along the walls were rows of kiosks, each of which advertised a destination and the list of stops in between. This hanger in down-town Athens was Greek for the Greeks, with no concessions to foreign speakers, even though the sign at the entrance had deigned to show an English translation. I walked along the line of kiosks, trying to make sense of their alphas and betas and gammas and deltas. Come on, I said to myself, you can do it. Remember Mr. Thalassos. Capitals are easier to pick out than lower case letters, and just before I came to the last kiosk, I looked up and saw in bold letters the word NAUPLION. I confidently paid for a ticket and soon found the right bus, back in the dark hanger, where the driver was busy stowing luggage into the boot. There were boxes tied up with string, sacks of potatoes, cardboard suitcases, a few leather ones, soldier's kit-bags (Greece still had conscription), and a duck in a wire cage. The driver indicated that I could go into the bus, so I climbed up and found my seat, number 21. Minutes later, an enormous woman heaved herself up the steps and started gesticulating. She became very angry and pointed to my seat. Her voice was rising alarmingly, when a male passenger explained to me, in English, that the seat numbers indicated the position in front, not the one behind. I hurriedly moved forward, mollifying the irate woman, and all was peace again. The driver shut the boot, then clambered in, and the bus moved out of the dim garage and into the daylight, carefully negotiating the exit road, which was no more than an alley and barely wider than the width of the vehicle itself.

We were soon enmeshed again with the screaming trucks and the voluble drivers, and I resigned myself to a less than pleasant half hour, while we were still in the worst of the traffic. Then, something happened that transported me back a couple of thousand years (a common phenomenon in Greece). Beside one factory, I saw a sign to ELEUSIS. Beautiful young men used to walk along the Sacred Way from Athens to the temple of Elefsis, and there partake of its mysteries, which they were bound on pain of death never to divulge. Many writers have tried to uncover these mysteries but have never fully succeeded. Some believe they were essentially a tribute to the corn goddess, Demeter, but this has never been confirmed. The sign was fixed to the railings of the factory, and, as we passed, I could see that the floor behind was covered with oil and clinker. Even Demeter could not have transformed it into a field of corn with waving poppies.

The traffic became less dense as the bus drove out of Athens and towards Piraeus, and then, round a bend, there came another transportation into the Greek past! I saw the sea, the blue Aegean, with the island of Salamis in the distance. Was I ever going to shake off these pervasive old stories? More to the point, did I want to? During the war against the Persians, the enemy's ships were bearing down upon Athens, but the smaller Greek fleet hid behind the island of Salamis and, at a critical moment, took the Persians by surprise and defeated them, fulfilling the words of the Delphic oracle, who prophesied that Athens would be saved by "a wooden wall", meaning, of course, the wooden Greek triremes. The bus driver carried on, oblivious to the intrusions of history, and followed the contours of the shore. I lay back in my seat, tired but blissful; the sun nudged through the curtained windows, intensifying the smell of the sea and the people-smell of garlic, sweat and warm bread. The angry woman behind me was gently snoring and I, too, dropped off, dreaming of white horses in green meadows. Then, turning to stretch a cramped leg, I opened my eyes and saw the outline of a town in the distance. Nafplion already? I must have slept longer than I realised. Still fuzzy from sleep, I asked my neighbour,

"Nafplion?"

"*Ochi* (no)", he said. "Corinthos."

We were hardly half way! The bus stopped at the modern

town of Corinth, which had grown up away from the ancient site, and three quarters of the passengers decamped, very few new ones replacing them. New Corinth is a dump; just rows of undistinguished houses, small cramped shops, and the so-called bus station, which was at the back of a café. The place reminded me of a Welsh mining village during the depression, albeit with sunshine. Where had the bulk of the passengers gone? Was there a more up-market area away from the bus-stop, or was this it? More worrying, was this going to be it for the rest of the journey? Had I made a dreadful mistake? Perhaps I had been too hasty in scorning the attractions of Athens.

I now discovered that our next stop, which was only a few kilometres out of Corinth, was the official half-way break. The bus clattered over a metal bridge, rather like the Bailey bridges that were thrown across rivers in WW11, and drew up at a decent sized restaurant and service station, far better than the dump we had just left. We got out to stretch our legs, and my fuddled brain suddenly became clearer. That wasn't any old bridge, that was the entrance to the Peloponnese; and below it wasn't any old river; but the Corinth Canal. Would there be time for me to nip back and see it? Using my phrase book; I asked the driver.

"*Posi ora?*"

He held up his fingers to indicate that we had twenty minutes.

The Corinth Canal is an unassuming ditch, which has transformed the Peloponnese from an isthmus to an island and enabled ships to pass from the Aegean to the Ionian sea. The result makes economic sense, and even the Emperor Nero, in Roman times, had spotted this, but his ideas foundered at the planning stage. It took the French, more than two thousand years later, to complete it. I leaned over the metal barrier and looked down at the surface of the water below. The narrow width played with the perspective and made the drop seem immense. Had this place been a lure for suicides, I wondered, like Waterloo Bridge or that Japanese crater? I watched a passing ship gliding slowly southward through the straight, like an animated toy. Would one of those modern cruise ships be able to get through? I doubted it. There was a warning hoot from the coach, and I realised that the minutes had flown, and I needed to have a pee.

"*Pou einai touleta?*"

An attendant gave me a piece of toilet paper the size of a woman's handkerchief, and I went into a cubicle. Toilets in rural Greece are a hole in the ground, with a serrated slab on either side on which to place the feet. If you are a woman, you have to squat, or risk spraying your clothes. That's for peeing. I refused to visualise the manoeuvres necessary for crapping. As I was carefully straightening up, there was another hoot from the bus, and I hurriedly returned, avoiding the impatient glares of the passengers, and trying not to listen to the sniffy comments from my fat friend. The Corinth Canal had been disappointing. I felt that more could have been done to make us aware of it, and the same went for modern Corinth. The old city was so near, yet very little information was given about it. How many travellers had passed it by, unaware of the Pierian Spring, or the stone from which St. Paul had preached, during the eighteen months he lived there? Indeed, the whole area was ripe for a bit more hype. Maybe a PR whiz-kid should be put on the job. Then, I laughed at myself. Here was I, advocating the very measures that would attract the tourists I had taken such pains to avoid!

By now it was midday, siesta time, but the bus driver carried on regardless. As a concession to his sleepy passengers, he toned down the volume of his cassette player, so that the strains of a Cretan dance by Theodorakis were pleasantly soothing. The passengers sweltered. There were snores from some of them. Women fluttered their fans, ineffectively moving the hot air around. A baby wailed. In the towns, the shops had drawn down their blinds; the streets of the villages were empty; the tractors were silent. I crouched behind the pleated curtains, trying to keep away from the searing, penetrating sun. I was hot, hot, hot, and very tired, having been travelling for more than sixteen hours. When we came to Argos, not even the shades of Agamemnon could rouse me from my weariness. Again, I was tempted to think that the whole enterprise was a mistake. Surely, a prolonged treatment of cortisone would have done just as well. I decided that, when we eventually arrived at Nafplion, I would symbolically paddle in the Argonic Gulf, have a good meal and a sleep, then get on the next bus and go back home to Wales. But this was not to be, because leaving Argos, we crossed some railway lines and joined a long, straight road with eucalyptus trees on either side. I was drawn by them to the horizon, eight miles away, and, as I wearily raised my eyes, I saw etched across the sky the jagged outline of a Venetian castle. It was a thing of wonder, even in my debilitated state, and as my companion, who had boarded the bus at Argos, noticed my astonishment, he said quietly, with local pride,

"Palamidi."

Although I didn't realise it at the time, that edifice was going to be the backdrop to many of my adventures in the future. A few minutes later, the bus drew up at the main square of Nafplion, and as I eased my stiff legs, I hoped the town was sophisticated enough to have a sit-down loo. It was now 2.30pm. If I could find a modest hotel, I might be able to begin my search for an estate agent after tea. I remembered the words of my ex-husband.

"My wife is an irritating woman, but I'll say this for her, she doesn't give up easily."

Chapter 3

Palamidi

I looked around at the town that I had only previously seen as a dot on the map. In spite of the blight of Corinth, my expectations were high. Would they be fulfilled? Nafplion seemed immolated in the searing afternoon heat. The leaves hung limply on the trees. A small dustcart with no driver was parked in the shade. In front of the bus station, a kiosk remained open, selling sweets and cigarettes, but the attendant sat outside, dozing, his panama hat covering his face. Nothing stirred, only a rangy cat scavenged listlessly around the base of the rubbish cart. I shouldered my bag and set off along a small cobbled street, which seemed to lead to the main part of the town. It was lined with shops, most of which had their blinds drawn. The balconies above were festooned with bougainvillea, interspersed with pots of brilliant red geraniums, teetering precariously near the edges of the balustrades. A sleek black cat emerged from a doorway and scampered to the other side of the road. My feet echoed on the cobbles, and I wished that I had worn quieter shoes. Then, the little street opened out into a large square, and the cobbles were exchanged for rather splendid pink marble slabs. I found out later that this was Syntagma (Constitution) Square, not, of course, like the famous one in Athens but, in its way, very interesting, with its mixture of building styles. On one side there was an imposing seventeenth century edifice, which must have been Venetian (the Venetians had ruled that part of Greece off and on for several hundred years). Opposite this was a mosque ornamented with Arabic tracery, which now seemed to be functioning as a cinema, while behind its onion dome loomed the clock tower of the Cathedral of St. George. These two religious rivals stood there, set immutably in stone and bright in the slanting afternoon sun. One corner of the square was occupied by a large café, its tables and chairs spilled out on to the marble paving stones and were protected from the sun's glare by a striped canopy. Up some steps and next to a small bookshop was a large chunk of stone on which was carved the life-sized relief of a lion. Lions in Greece? Maybe, I would find out about it later.

As I stood there pondering, a church bell struck three times, to be followed by several others in the town. At the last stroke, a waiter in a long white apron came out of the café and started to wipe down the marble tabletops. At the same time, the owner of the bookshop began to pull up his blinds.

"*Yassou, Tassis,*" he called to the waiter. Tassis answered with a wave of his hand.

The town was gently stirring. Maybe now was the time to find a modest hotel that would welcome a visitor. Leaving the square, I went down another alley, opposite to the one from which I had entered, but, unhappily, I saw that it was full of tourist shops. Had I really shaken off the invasive European tourists? Would the evening echo to hilarity and plate-smashing, even here? Between a *pharmacia* (chemist) and a souvenir shop, I saw a small hotel, and, peering tentatively through the window, I made out a group of men drinking coffee and watching television. I started to climb up the several steps to the entrance, and then hesitated. What was I doing there, for God's sake, a woman alone in a foreign country and hardly able to put together one sentence of the language? I forced myself to carry on up into the lobby, and, as I entered, the murmur of conversation stopped and half a dozen pairs of brown eyes turned to look at me. There was a momentary hush, and then one man detached himself from the group and went over to the reception desk. He was dark and handsome, with a truly magnificent moustache.

"*Kalispera*," he said.

"*Kalispera*," I replied, and then, bravely, "*thelo, thelo, ena, ena...*"

He smiled. "You want a room?" He spoke English!

"Yes, please, for three nights."

He took a key from the shelf and picked up my bag. I followed him to the lift. The remaining men sighed, their curiosity satisfied, and went back to the television screen, but as I went up in the lift, I fancied that one of them laughed. The room was clean, with a shower and a sit-down toilet; there was even a bidet! I immediately undressed and showered away the sweat and dust of the last twenty-four hours, then washed my underclothes in the bidet and hung them out to dry. I leaned over the balcony, breathing in the cool air. It was soft and comforting, unlike the smog of Athens. On the other side of the road was a grocery and vegetable shop, which had already raised its blinds, and outside it sat the proprietor, an elderly man in a dark suit and a trilby hat, nursing a black fluffy cat. I was beginning to realise that cats in Greece were the equivalent of dogs in the U.K. but being more independent, they did not allow themselves to be so pampered. The man looked more like a teacher than a shopkeeper, a retired teacher perhaps, maybe even a mathematics teacher, like I had been. Maybe we could chat about schools we had known. Then I pulled myself back to reality; I hadn't been able to reply to the fat woman at the bus station in Athens. How could I converse with a strange shopkeeper? I settled for giving him a smile, when I went out to look round the town. He smiled back, still stroking his cat.

Nafplion is a rocky peninsula town, leaning over into the Gulf of Argos, with a shoreline of around twenty kilometres. It is a natural harbour and has been known as such since Neolithic times. From the shore, several alleys lead up to the main town, where the shops and squares and municipal parks are found. They are on level ground, but soon the rock takes over, and tier upon tier of white-washed houses climb up to the fortress of Palamidi, that jagged outline that I had first seen when the bus left Argos. Its walls seem to grow out of the living rock as they spread across the summit and dominate the town below. The rock, 216 metres high, has always had great strategic value, and has been captured many times, by the Byzantines, the Greeks, the Venetians, the Turks, and the Venetians again. The last time the Venetians occupied it, in the early eighteenth century, they decided to strengthen it, and they built the fortress that we now call Palamidi. Unhappily for them, the Turks re-conquered the fortress a year later, and kept it for the next two hundred years, when they themselves were ousted by the Greeks in the War of Independence. The Greeks have had it ever since, except for a blip in WW11, when it was occupied by the Germans.

Palamidi towers above Nafplion and no part of the town is free from its shadow. Turn any corner and that dark shape looms ahead, menacing or protective, depending on the mood of the viewer. Equally, there is no getting away from the statues of the *palikares* (heroes) of the Independence war. They are mostly in the centres of small parks, usually with the nearby streets named after them. Among them are Kolokotronis and his comrade, Staicopulous, both *kelphtic* (guerrilla) warriors.

Staicopulous stands, in traditional costume, at the base of Palamidi. Kolokotronis, wearing a classical Greek helmet and the same traditional short skirt as Staicopulous, is mounted astride a horse. Do the same speculations apply to those short skirts as they do to our Scottish Highlanders' kilts? The statue of Kapodistro, the first president of Independent Greece, is more soberly dressed in a morning suit. He was a statesman more than a *palikari*, but he died a warrior's death, assassinated in the Church of St. Spiridon, behind Syntagma Square. There were women fighters in the War of Independence, among them a sea captain called Boubulina. She fought many battles against the Turks, and her statue is down by the harbour. Being woman, she only merits a bust, but as it faces out to the Gulf of Argos, she has the best view.

Night falls early in the Mediterranean, and as I stepped out, the blue sky deepened to navy and the streets lights came on. However, the shops, even the post office, stayed open, and I saw family groups picking their way over the cobbles; mother, father, children, black-clothed grandmothers, all taking a turn round the alleys and squares and the two main shopping streets. The adults gossiped and window-gazed and the children ate ice-cream, but, for the moment, I was not interested in studying local mores because I was on a mission. Back at the hotel, the man with the moustache had told me that the Greek for estate agent was *kteematomezitee,* and so I set off to look for this absurd word. There were plenty of signs on hoardings and above shop windows but nothing approximating to this Greek word. I counted four wedding shops, showing white dresses in silks and laces and taffetas; a shop with a lighting display very similar to the one I had passed near Hadrian's arch in Athens, and several hardware shops selling tools and bottled gas, but no *kteematomezitee*. At the fourth wedding shop window, I idly pondered on the phenomenon of countries like Greece, with macho cultures. I supposed that young women insisted on adhering to traditional weddings and all the trappings because betrothal and marriage ceremonies were the only times in their lives when they were allowed any respect. As the stars came out, whole families finished their stroll and sat down in the outside cafés, to drink ouzo and black coffee, eat sweet honey cakes, and slurp ice cream served in tall glasses. They sat in the lamplight and chatted, chatted incessantly and sipped their boiling hot coffee in the Turkish manner. Although, after Independence, the Greeks tried to obliterate the three-hundred-year-old Turkish presence by turning their mosques into cinemas or razing them to the ground for car parks, vestiges of the old culture persist: an efficient drainage system, fountains, ice cream, and cups of sweet black coffee, made in a long handled pot called a *briki*. But, woe betide any foreigner who asks for a Turkish coffee in a Greek restaurant.

I was tired. I had found no *kteematomezitees,* written up either in Greek or Roman alphabets. My body was telling me that it needed food and rest and, anyway, the sea was beckoning. I went to a harbour restaurant and looked through the menu:

> *Taramasalata* (smoked fish roe)
> *Dolmades* (stuffed vine leaves)
> *Keftedes* (meat balls)
> *Omeleta*
> *Mousaka* (shepherds pie)

I ordered omelette. Experiments with Greek cuisine could wait until next day. The sea was calm, little waves gently lapping against the sea wall, just as they had on that night I spent with Costas beside the Saronic Gulf. Are all Greek seas like millponds? What about Odysseus battling home from Troy, or did he invent the storms as an excuse to pacify his wife Penelope? Agamemnon was holed up in Aulis because the seas were too rough for his fleet to sail. He made the fatal mistake of sacrificing his daughter to the sea gods, to encourage them to calm the waters, and it worked, but Homer lets us know that he got his come-uppance ten years later, when he went home after the war. His furious wife, Clytemnestra, drowned him in the bath. I've always been drawn to that story. It gave me great satisfaction to know that, three thousand years ago, a gutsy woman was prepared to buck the macho trend of the so-called heroes.

Drunk with the balmy air and the lights winking on the water, I ordered a glass of ouzo to celebrate my arrival. Ouzo comes as a clear liquid and, when water is added, it turns milky and has the kick of a mule. Sipping the drink, I finished my omelette, sat back in the cane armchair and looked at the seascape. A little way off shore was the islet fortress of Bourtzi. It is no bigger than a car park, a miniature Palamidi, but much more ancient, having been built five hundred years before its dominant rival. As I listened to the conversation of the other patrons around me, I wondered how long it would be before the sounds emerged as comprehensible words. I was afraid it would be many months before I could go into a local store and ask for a pint of milk. I continued to sip my drink, relishing the aniseed taste, and looking out at the ageless sea. Then, I saw a medium sized yacht gliding by from left to right and slowly disappearing over the horizon. I watched it fascinated and, just as it disappeared from sight, I realised with a shock that it had BLACK SAILS.

There is the story of King Aegeus of Athens, waiting on a high part of the Acropolis for the return of his son Theseus from Crete. Theseus had promised his father that, if the expedition went well, he would change the black sails on his ship for white ones. Nearing Greece and sailing past Sounion, and full of his various successes: slaying the Minotaur, seducing umpteen women, he forgot to do this. Aegeus, seeing the black sails, believed his son was dead, and threw himself from the battlements. Remembering the old tale, I felt an uncanny sense of foreboding, but put it down to the unaccustomed ouzo.

"Come on, you're letting your imagination run away with you!"

I left the restaurant and prepared myself for tomorrow's blitz on the estate agents of Nafplion, wherever they happened to be lurking. Over the years, I went to that restaurant many times, but I never saw the black sails again.

Chapter 4

Gregory

Nafplion, along with most towns washed by the
Mediterranean, wakes up early and I followed suit. I
opened my window and smelled freshly baked bread, but when
I peered through the leaves of the bougainvillaea to the grocery
shop opposite, I saw that it was still closed. Although I was
anxious to get going in my search for that elusive estate agent,
I thought it wise to wait until the local businesses had opened
up, I was also hungry, so I walked the few steps to the café in
Syntagma Square and ordered toast and *ena Nescafé*. I sat under
the awning and watched the town come to life. The portly
owner of the bookshop rolled open his shutters and took in the
bundle of papers that had been dumped on his doorstep;
schoolboys with satchels ran past, tearing off pieces of crusty
bread; a crocodile of prim schoolgirls crossed the square on
their way to Mass; at the far end, a workman with paint-
streaked overalls called across to the bookshop owner,

"*Kalimera, Kirios Philippos. Pos pragmata?*" (How are things?)

Mr. Philippos, with a shrug and an upward jerk of his head,
which is Greek for negative, indicated that things were not too
good. Soon, smartly dressed women clip-clopped across to the
business part of the town, dodging the children, who were

bouncing balls on the marble slabs, even though a notice expressly forbade it. I recognised the word *anagorevmenos* (forbidden) from my phrase book. If ever I arranged to have a car in Greece, it would be a useful word to remember. I buttered the toast and spread it with the apricot jam they provided. Jam at breakfast, how bizarre! Now I knew that I was in a foreign country! Then, I spun out the time by ordering another cup of coffee. A man at the next table bought a newspaper, *Ta Nea,* from the bookshop and settled down to read it. I dallied with my second cup as long as I dared, then went to the bookshop myself, to buy a map of Nafplion and continue my search from the previous evening.

Following the map, I started along Lamprinido Street, and turned right into Constantinou Street. But, hang on, King Constantine had been given his marching orders years ago, even though he still hob-nobbed with our own Royal Family! Perhaps the street had been named after the earlier Constantinou. Next, I went along Zigoma Avenue and on to Kapidostria Square, where the statue of the first Prime Minister, resplendent in a nineteenth century tail coat, gazed purposefully ahead. And then, behold, I found myself walking down Boubulinas Street. So, the Lady Pirate hadn't been completely neglected, but I noticed that her bust wasn't marked on the map. That would have been too much for the City Fathers to stomach. Re-crossing Syntagma from the south, I noticed that the man with the newspaper was still there, so I needn't have hurried with my second cup after all. I looked closer as I passed near him, and saw that he had got to the crossword. A Greek crossword would certainly be something to aim for! Three across. A coffee pot, beginning with "b", 5 letters.

Whoa, I really must stop this, I hadn't travelled two thousand miles to fantasise in the sun, I had a mission to carry out, fruitless though it had been so far. I carried on doggedly, looking in shop windows, peering down steps into dark office entrances, trying to decipher brass plates, but found nothing that approximated to the Greek word for an estate agent. I even tried enquiring from passers-by.

"Parakalo. Pou einai ena kteema-tomez-itees?" (Please, where is an estate agent?)

I received blank stares, or that upward nod that denotes all things negative; or even worse, eyes that followed me curiously down the street. Maybe I wasn't asking for an estate agent; maybe the man behind the bar had given me the wrong word; maybe I was asking for something unsavoury. I felt suddenly very vulnerable, and needed to get away from people and public places and find anonymity in some small café, where I could review my situation.

I dived down the nearest alleyway but there was no sign of a welcoming café, just a lingerie shop at the top, and a peculiar smell coming from the bottom. I was about to turn back, when I spotted a hanging sign swinging from a neat looking window. It was in English!

GREGORY PETRULAKIS.
LAND AND PROPERTY DEVELOPER

Another Eureka! Hardly daring to breathe, I pressed the doorbell, but there was no answer; the place was shut. What did I expect? Miracles for the Israelites only came one at a time, so who was I to merit better treatment? It was enough that I had found my *kteema-tomez-itees* at last. I peered through the modern slatted blinds and wondered where he was. Where was Mr. Petrulakis? Out with a theodolite and a clip board maybe, measuring a piece of land. Perhaps, it would have been my piece of land, if I had only got there sooner; but by now someone else had it. The deal was probably being sealed at this very moment and, in all likelihood, it had been sold to a

German. Was it a big piece? Could I buy half of it from the German? Would I like a German neighbour? Well, if the Greeks could accept them, after all the Nazis had done, perhaps I could be magnanimous, too. I stood back and looked again at the swinging sign, and tried to visualise Mr. Petrulakis. Was he a solid businessman, like Mr. Manolis in Queensway, or was he a youngster just starting out? It is said that you can judge a man by the company he keeps, so, who else had shops in the alley?

Opposite was a dry cleaner, who was pressing a pair of trousers between two padded boards. I recognised the toxic smell as the steam rose up. Next door was a picture-framer with a shop window full of gold-encrusted frames around pictures of the Virgin Mary, and at the end of the alley, which terminated in two bollards, was a butcher's shop. The owner was busy chopping a shoulder of mutton in half over a scrubbed tree stump, and the sight of the blood coupled with the smell from the dry cleaners made me want to heave, but I could hardly blame Gregory for that. (May I call you Gregory?) Just as I was scribbling a note to push under the door, a car drew up and stopped with a jerk, just two inches away from the nearest bollard. The driver came smiling towards me.

"*Kalimera*," I said.

"Good morning," he replied in English, and I knew that this was the second miracle.

He was taller than most Greeks, with less of an olive skin than was usual. In fact, he looked very English, except that an Englishman would not have greeted a prospective client, while at the same time eating a Mars bar. My instincts should have warned me, but my defences were down and I over-rode any doubts as to his character.

"Enter," he said and engulfed my hand in his.

We went into his *grafio* (office) and I felt him looking at me, just as Mr. Manolis had done, but sideways this time. Maybe it's a Greek tic. The office was new, with freshly painted white walls; hanging on them were two imposing certificates and several photographs of houses. The tubular furniture was recent and he had a telephone and a fax machine on his desk.

"Please sit down." he said. "How can I help you? Would you like some coffee?"

"Well Mr. – er – Petrulakis," I babbled.

He smiled and said, "Call me Gregory."

"Well..." I hesitated. I had come so far, been so near disappointment, wrestled with so many doubts... "I want to buy a house in Greece," I blurted out.

"For yourself?"

I had a sense of unreality, this was a re-run of that first interview in Queensway. He took out a slim ledger from the desk drawer and traced down a list with his finger, pausing at times to look at me, then he stopped at one entry, which seemed to satisfy him.

"I have a flat in Tolon," he said.

"Tolon?"

"It's a seaside town near here."

I had come to Greece with a very clear idea of where I didn't want to live: Athens, as you know, and any complex dominated by the English Brigade. I wanted to subsume myself into the Greek mores, integrate as far as possible with the community. A flat in a seaside town? It sounded doubtful. Wasn't Tolon the place the package tourists were going to when our plane landed in Athens? Gregory was looking at me expectantly.

"I – I don't know," I said.

"I think you'll like it."

Oh well, I had to begin somewhere, so I got into his car and we headed off eastwards, passing through orange groves and fields of tobacco plants. Tolon is an unabashed tourist venue. From a wide sandy beach, new hotels and apartments rise up in tiers, replicating the terraces at Nafplion, but without their charm. The only street, which hugs the shore, is full of shops selling gewgaws, beach equipment and yesterday's European papers. A restaurant on the corner where the street swings round to a more prosaic supermarket and a wet fish shop, advertises "Inglish Breakfast". The third floor flat that Gregory showed me seemed reasonable enough, with a balcony that faced directly on to the sea, but the walls were paper-thin, no bulwark against jolly holidaymakers next door, who were unlikely to be Greek. How could my dreams of integration flourish in such a setting? Gregory was doing his salesman bit. Was I interested? Didn't I find the view spectacular?

"And they tell me that the supermarket sells English tea," he added, as a final touch.

When we got back into the car and he looked at me hopefully.

"I'm sorry, it's not what I am looking for," I said.

Gregory pursed his lips and banged in the clutch, jerking the car forward, and we drove in silence for the next few miles. Then, the professional salesman took over from the modern day Achilles. He slowed down a little, took a deep breath and said mildly,

"What exactly in mind do you have?" his English slipping a little.

I tried to make him understand that I wanted to be in touch with real people, real country people. I wanted to learn their language, understand their life, gradually feel accepted by them. He said nothing and I wondered if he understood what I was getting at. After all, I was speaking what to him was a foreign language, and even though he was obviously very fluent, he couldn't be expected to catch on to its various nuances. On the other hand, it was more than likely that he was still in a sulk. Suddenly, he swung savagely off the main road and turned into a smaller one, and I began to feel a little nervous. A few Greek roads are of Autobahn standard, but the secondary ones are not so good, and there are others which it doesn't seem to be anyone's responsibility to maintain. This was one of those. We bumped along through a small village and came to the outskirts of an even smaller one. Then, the road petered out and was swallowed up in sweet smelling bracken. Gregory stopped the car, skipped round to the passenger's side, ushered me out and, with a flourish, pointed to a patch of waste ground.

"What do you think?" he asked proudly.

I was momentarily confused as I looked at the empty space. Where were the theodolite and the clipboard? Where was the German?

"Well?" urged Gregory.

The scenery was magnificent. Orange groves lined one side, and gnarled olive trees climbed up a steep incline on the other. In front was the plain of Argos, the ancient kingdom of Agamemnon, with the hills of Mycenae a blur in the distance. I caught my breath. Did I smell thyme? Of course. It was endemic here, grey clumps of it in the rocks, redolent of country kitchens.

"Well?" he said again.

I turned to him regretfully, remembering my experience with the unaffordable properties in Queensway. Perhaps he had made the same mistake as Mr. Manolis when judging my financial situation.

"I'm sorry, but it would be quite beyond my means to build a house here."

Gregory seemed undaunted and drove back to the office as if he were on a high. He brought out maps and specifications of the proposed house, spreading them over the desk and spilling them onto to the floor.

"It's a new technique," he said. "Flat pack houses." Where had he got the jargon from? B&Q? "The sections come from Athens," he continued, "as pre-formed concrete blocks."

He pulled out a brochure from under several architects' drawings."How many bedrooms do you want? Two? That'll be, let's see," he attacked the calculator, "hm, no more than a largish flat in Tolon. I would say around £20,000."

I was tempted. A white house, it would have to be white, set among orange and olive groves and looking out over the plain of Argos. I would be re-populating a barren piece of land in the Peloponnese, re-populating because, thousands of years earlier, others had surely been there.

"I'll think about it," I told Gregory, but he knew and I knew that I was already hooked.

Next day, on the bus ride back to Athens, I was in a dream; even New Corinth seemed to have acquired some charm. This was no dream, however, but a reality on a bare hillside. Why was it bare? I looked through the bus window at the ripples from Salamis lapping softly up to the shore. The bareness was something to do with the lie of the land, nothing to worry about. Everyone knows that Greece is a rocky country.

Chapter 5

The journey back to Wales was uneventful, leaving me with plenty of thinking time, and my brain raced backwards and forwards. I was not yet committed but all my instincts impelled me to go forward. There were doubts, of course; was I over-reaching myself both in scope and money? Could I trust Gregory? Was I about to make a colossal mistake? Jones the Taxi picked me up from the little station in Powys and drove me the last three miles to our village. My home was the central one of three former farm labourers' cottages, the last to be gentrified. I had bought it cheaply after I sold my place in London, and it was the profit from this transaction that had enabled me to think of buying a house in Greece. In mid-Wales, I wasn't exactly an English newcomer, because I had been born and brought up in the mining valleys in the south, but the locals still viewed me with a certain amount of suspicion. My neighbour, Gareth, was clipping his hedge when I got out of the taxi, and he addressed me in hybrid Welsh.

"You're back. *Sut oedd Groeg?*" (How was Greece?)

"*Eitha da, diolch,*" (Alright, thank you) I answered cautiously. Gareth was a well known gossip.

"*Dych chi wedi prynu rhywbeth?*" (Did you buy anything?)

How did he know my reason for going to Greece! "Not yet," I said tersely, and went into the house.

I didn't sleep well that night; due to jet lag, of course, but the next night was the same, and the next. On the third morning,

I got up ragged and irritable and determined to put an end to the mood swings that had been plaguing me. I went down to the local post office and sent a fax to Gregory.

Fax to Gregory: **I have decided to buy the house. Confirm.**

After I had given in the form, I felt more relaxed than I had been for days.

"There's excitement for you!" said Doris-the-post.

The next few months were fraught, punctuated by faxes winging to and fro.

Fax from Gregory:	Do you want the windows facing south or east?
Reply from me:	East. Facing Argos.
Fax from Gregory:	I have to pay the surveyor.
Reply from me:	Cheque in the post.
Fax from Gregory:	Do you want the inside walls panelled?
Reply from me:	How much extra will it cost?

As the months went by, I was on tenterhooks. I knew houses don't spring up overnight, even B&Q houses, but waiting for the delivery period was unsettling. Added to which, I realised that knowledge picked up from classical texts, and a twenty-year-ago flutter with a Greek sailor were not enough to see me through the coming social hurdles. There was, for example, *philotimo*, the Greek term for love of honour. Rather like the Catholic Inquisition, terrible things have been done in its name, and even today, young women have been killed for besmirching the purity of the family. Of course, in the bigger cities, like Athens or Salonica, the obsession is diluted, but it is still rife in the villages, and dominates society. The hot Greek sun doesn't help, of course, as the poet Byron wryly observed:

What men call gallantry, and gods adultery
Is much more common when the climate's sultry.

But rules are made to be bent, and just as Welsh shepherds while away the midnight hour with a favourite sheep, rural Greeks are rumoured to use ripe pumpkins. All apocryphal, of course, but I remembered that a Cardingdon shepherd was arraigned in court for "bestiality" as recently as 1990! His defence was that he was just having a pee in the open air. But to return to my Greeks. The young men bent the rules, and homosexuality was one avenue for them to go down, but increasingly, with the advent of liberated women from Europe on holiday, they had an alternative means of exercising their testosterone, away from family pressure. I was excluded from all this nonsense by virtue of my advanced age, but I wasn't excluded from another problem, that of religion.

I have none myself and viewed most beliefs in a Divine Being with cynicism; and the sight of priests in Nafplion confirmed my aversion. They wore long, flowing, black robes, and black hats with flat crowns like pancakes, and they came in all shapes and sizes. Muscular young ones strode along, monopolising the pavements, middle aged ones nodded to passers-by with fake benignity, very ancient ones tottered along with aid of a silver-handled, ebony stick. I thought the oldest ones were probably retired, and then I thought again. Are priests allowed to retire? God never does, so why should they? I had passed six churches in my search for an estate agent; supposing that each church supported three priests, that made at least eighteen of them, and when I cased the town, they all seemed to be in various cafés, drinking coffee. What about lighting candles, and genuflecting, and giving to the poor? The office of priest in the Orthodox Church is ambiguous. His allegiance is to the Ecumenical Patriarchate of Constantinople, not the Pope in Rome. He takes no vows of celibacy – they leave that to the monks – and he is allowed to marry. Also, although he pays homage to the Christian virtues, he takes on the baggage of previous faiths, which are as old as the broken stones of antiquity. Added to this, he imbibes the persona of those ancient times, when priests were revered but also dreaded. Even today, he is distrusted and considered a harbinger of disaster, and to meet a priest in the street portends ill-luck. No wonder the pavements are kept clear for him. Paradoxically, he is held in awe. He officiates at weddings, funerals, the churching of women, and all other Christian festivals; at the same time, he walks the tightrope that crosses between modern faith and the superstitions of olden times. A further ambiguity is his role vis-à-vis women. Peasant women are particularly well known for their piety, which is largely rooted in ancient customs. It also serves to get them out of the house and draws them to the priest, who gives them the respect and attention that they do not experience from their macho husbands. This increases the general distrust and jealousy that men have against priests, but the men are caught in a bind. They can't overtly enter into a fight against Mother Church and her earthly representative, even though they'd often like to! I hoped that, if I kept a low profile and didn't blatantly show my colours as an unbeliever, I could avoid any misunderstanding associated with Greece and religion.

One other problem that kept me awake at night was that of integration. I wanted to integrate with the Greeks, but would they want to integrate with me? In 1921, the Greeks from Asia Minor were brutally expelled by the Turks, in some cases they were literally thrown into the sea. The Greek government of the day accepted the refugees into Northern Greece, but neglected to inform the local inhabitants, and the resentment lingers on, even into the twenty-first century. Although they speak the same language and have the same roots, the "newcomers" have still not been assimilated. As I sat in my cottage in Wales, I reflected on my own situation. How did I expect to be accepted into such a society, with my threefold disadvantages: a foreigner, a woman, and a single woman, as well? I would have to tread warily.

I carried on with my preparations; trips to London for Greek lessons, forms to be signed, money transferred, car insurance, power of attorney, but as the weeks stretched out and turned into months, the house seemed to be getting no nearer. When would it change from being a fanciful sketch on a page and turn into a house I could live in? Then, one morning, Doris handed me a fax.

Fax from Gregory: **The lorry is bringing your house from Athens this afternoon.**

"Duw, duw," said Doris, "a house in Greece and on a lorry too. There's fancy!"

I walked around proudly that day. Not many people have a house being transported for them from Athens. A week went by and there was no more word from Gregory, no reassuring questions about sites, no more requests for money, I felt the dream slipping away. I sent a fax.

Fax from me: **What is happening?**
Reply from Gregory: **Everything going well.**

I didn't believe him. Maybe it had been an elaborate confidence trick, operated by the Greek Mafia. I looked at my bank statements. Yes, all the cheques had been cashed. Was Gregory in the Bahamas by now, lolling on the beach with a floozy? Dropping all my commitments, I took another cheap return from Heathrow. Knowing the ropes this time, I arrived by bus at Nafplion with daylight to spare. Gregory met me, proving that at least he hadn't scarpered yet, and we drove to the spot. As we got nearer, I was trembling with excitement, waiting to arrive at that last bend, when the house would be revealed, rising up from the patch of ground that I had bought so many months ago. It was a great disappointment. Half assembled, with no doors or windows, and still a dull grey colour, it was a blot on the landscape. I looked at the houses of the neighbouring farms, with their whitewashed walls, cool verandas covered with vine leaves, cats lying in the sun, olive trees, all that I had hoped for and hadn't got.

"You should have waited a little longer," said Gregory. He squeezed my arm.

"Don't worry, we're going to have it painted. Trust me, it will look beautiful. How many steps do you want up to the veranda?"

Mollified, I allowed him to take me back to Nafplion. As we drove through the next village, he pointed to a small turning.

"That's where I live, down there."

"Alone?"

"No, with my mother and father."

So, he wasn't married! Where did that leave me? Could I assume that my age would protect me from that fabled Greek testosterone? It depended how desperate he became, I supposed.

"What's the name of your village?" I asked, masking my anxiety.

"Agios Varnova. St. Barnabas to you."

"And my place?"

"Profitis Elias."

The prophet Elijah. Wasn't he the one who went up to heaven in a chariot? Now I had the edge on Gregory; a prophet is much more important than a saint. I discovered later that the name was far from unique; all over Greece, assorted hills commemorate the ascent of that holy charioteer.

I stayed in the same hotel in the tourist street that night, and the man at the bar remembered me, which was gratifying. Nevertheless, in spite of Gregory's promises, I was disappointed about the house. The following afternoon, I took a Staithos taxi to look at it alone, without my mentor hovering. I walked around the unfenced patch and realised that I could just see the sea from the highest point. One wish was fulfilled anyway, but that dun-coloured monster still upset me. Yes, it was unfinished, I argued; yes, I had come to view it too soon, and, yes, I must give it more time, but I remained despondent as I walked back to the waiting taxi. The sun was now quite low and it would soon sink behind the top row of olive trees. Then, as I was about to get into the back seat of the cab, I stopped and listened. I heard a sound, light and pure, as if someone were playing a reed flute. The sound came nearer. Was it Pan himself? Then I saw, coming slowly round the bend, not the river god but an old shepherd leading a flock of sheep. He was playing on the type of bamboo flute that I had seen selling for a few drachmas in the local market, and behind him about forty sheep padded softly, their fleeces pink-tipped from the setting sun. I stood transfixed until the pageant passed out of sight and the music was absorbed by the quiet hills. Was it a mirage? I thought of Shakespeare's lines and silently mouthed them.

"The Isle is full of noises."

The taxi-driver coughed politely and broke my reverie. What was this foreigner doing, gazing into nothingness and talking to herself? He was missing a more lucrative fare, who was waiting for him in Nafplion. We drove back to town, with the sun behind us, and that night I slept well for first time for months.

The next morning, I had an appointment with Gregory. There were official papers to sign before I was due to catch the bus to the airport, and the schedule was tight. He wasn't in the office but the door was open. Inside was a priest, a flat-top, sitting in the visitor's chair and drinking coffee. His voluminous black robe was slightly hitched up, showing black scuffed shoes and black nylon socks. Did priests buy houses? Surely the church did all that secular stuff for them, leaving them free for their pastoral work, including, of course, drinking coffee. I stepped into the office and there was a pause.

"*Kalimera,*" I said tentatively.

"*Kalimera,*" said his reverence, and held out a hand.

How do you greet a priest? Curtsey, kiss his ringed finger, maybe make a sign to ward off the evil eye? I played safe and shook the proffered hand. There was a long silence and I wondered if I had done the wrong thing and offended him, but then I realised that he had no English. By then, my imperfect Greek had deserted me, so I spent the waiting time glancing sideways at him and studying his cherubic face. Pink cheeked and free of wrinkles, even though he must have been in his late sixties, this was obviously a contented man who lived well. A few minutes later, Gregory rushed into the office and apologised for being late.

"I asked Pappa Yannis to sit in for me," he explained.

Then, with a gesture, he introduced me to his father, the priest.

Chapter 6

I was surprised, but also relieved. Knowing that Gregory's father was a priest quelled the doubts I was beginning to have. For example, the office was so new. How long had Gregory been in business? Were the photographs on the walls pictures of the actual houses he had dealt with, or had he bought the pictures by the yard from an agency? And those certificates; for all I knew, they were the Greek equivalent of O-Level examination passes. Then there was the business of sex, ever present and unresolved. Although Gregory had behaved impeccably so far, he was a Greek, after all, and I couldn't be sure that my age would protect me. More prosaically, the most recent doubt had been about the floor tiles. I had seen the specification and they were supposed to be marble.

Gregory: I suggest we use plastic tiles.
Me: Why not the marble ones?
Gregory: Too slippery. You could have a nasty accident.

Had this been deliberate cost-cutting? Gregory had given me an inclusive estimate of £20,000. Was he now trying to palm me off with a cheaper substitute for the floor? Was I in the process of being duped, and was there more to come? These doubts had been beginning to build up into a serious loss of confidence in his integrity, but the identification of Gregory's father as a priest dispelled my worries. Pappa Yannis, as the upholder of public morality, would not permit his son to be a shyster. I flew home contented. Gregory had promised that the house would be ready in three months' time, with all the documents cleared and the services connected. I would then be free to move in.

I secured a window seat on the flight back and, as the plane circled above the smog of Athens, I saw the Parthenon sinking into the murky atmosphere, like a swan drowning. Prompted by the view, my thoughts were full of the ugly duckling I had left behind. Would three months be enough to turn it into a swan?

"Did you have a good holiday?"

Dragged back to the present, I turned to my neighbour, a sun-burned, middle-aged woman. "Er, yes, thank you."

Amazing how the English open up after a good dollop of sun.

"You look sad," she said. "It's hard to leave, isn't it? Been to Greece before?" While I was composing an answer, the woman continued. "We're very lucky; we come every year with Thompsons. All the couriers know us, and the hotel people try to give us the best rooms. Just like home from home, my Kevin says. Did you go with Thompsons?"

Without waiting for my reply, she eased off her shoes.

"Trouble with taking them off, it's difficult to get them back on again. And now there's this charter flight syndrome; danger of thrombosis, they say. Kevin tells me I ought to wear surgical stockings, as a precaution, you know. You alone?"

"Yes, I'm alone," I said dismissively, and turned the pages of my book, hating myself as I did so. What was the matter with me? Why did I resent this intrusion? I saw that Kevin and his small daughter were sitting in the seats in front. There they were, three normal people coming back from a normal holiday. How could I tell them, good Socialist that I was, that soon I would be able to go to their playground at will, whereas they would have to start saving up again for next year? I was embarrassed and ashamed to admit how opulent my life had become.

Back in Wales, I began the final preparations. My car was a Mini hatchback, and I hoped to drive it across to Felixstowe in England, then catch a cross-channel ferry to Boulogne in France. This was before we had the Euro tunnel. From there, I would pick up an overnight train with car transport attached, which would deposit me in Italian Bologna. Then, I would be on my own, driving to the coast at Ancona, and, finally, I would take another ferry, across the Mediterranean to Greece and the Peloponnese. On the face of it, the journey seemed daunting, but it was summer, the weather was good, and there seemed to be a holiday atmosphere everywhere. On the spur of the moment, I invited my youngest daughter, Veronica, to join me, as the date of the journey fell within her university vacation.

Veronica had been in and out of universities like a yo-yo. At the first university, she read English but left after a year and a half because, she said, "It wasn't relevant to real life." She conned the next one into accepting her, where she intended to study psychology, but she left after a few terms because she couldn't get on with the statistics. Would she stay at this third one? I doubted it. To me, Veronica always seemed to be the eternal adolescent, which had its good side and also its bad side. The bad side was the irresponsibility, but the good side was her cheerful zest for life, which made her a pleasant travelling companion. How old was she? I was never quite sure. When they were children, the ages of my three daughters were in geometric progression, each twice the age of the other, 3, 6, 12. Time doesn't stand still, and that method of calculating no longer applied. At a guess, I would say that Veronica was in her early twenties.

I began to fill up the hatchback. The deal with Gregory included the provision of a fridge and a cooker, but I would have to bring everything else myself, or buy it in Greece. Accordingly, I filled the car to the brim, with the exception of the passenger seat, but I soon realised that the poor little Mini couldn't take it all. I was in despair. I would have to leave some essentials behind. Then, Veronica arrived, cheerful, glamorous and bossy.

"You've no idea how to pack," she said, and took my tottering edifice to pieces. "Put the heavy stuff in first and pad it with clothes and sheets. Then, stuff the shoes with knickers and socks, and wrap the cutlery with towels. Don't waste a spare inch of space."

I had to admit that my youngest could be very efficient when she was on form. I felt like saying that, if she was so good at sorting things out, why hadn't she managed the statistics when she was at that university, but, wisely, I didn't. I put down her mood swings to the fact that half the time she was stoned on some sort of drug or another. I supposed she had brought some of the stuff with her, but that wouldn't last long, and where could she get a supply in mid-Wales? It was lucky that we would be leaving within the week, before darling Veronica began making dubious enquiries. I watched her put the last few items in the neatly packed Mini. She had certainly made a good job of it, and I didn't have to leave anything behind. Veronica wasn't actually pretty; her nose was too long, but she had good teeth and long blond hair that reached down to her knees. Those golden locks might be an asset, somewhere along the 2000-mile journey.

One Wednesday in mid-August, having locked up the house and given the key to Gareth, we set off. Everything went to plan; we slept aboard the P & 0 car ferry while it crossed the channel and landed at Boulogne. The tables outside the cafés were occupied by foreigners, speaking French, and only then did I feel that we had really started. We ordered café latte and looked at each other with secret, congratulatory smiles. Then we watched the car being loaded on to the transporter, which would be pulled behind the passenger carriages. It was a double-decker affair, rather like the trailers full of new cars that I used to see rumbling along the trunk roads in Britain. There was a maximum height for the cars to be carried, above which they wouldn't fit in. For example, the transporter couldn't take a Land Rover, but there was no trouble with our Mini. Having seen the car loaded, there were several hours to kill, so we wandered up to the battlements overlooking the sea. As I looked towards the horizon, I felt the hairs standing up on the back of my neck. More than forty years ago, a German soldier had stood on that very spot and looked expectantly towards England. Hitler had even issued him with a life-jacket! I didn't say anything to Veronica because the young find any mention of WW2 somewhat tiresome.

"We'll have to stock up with food," said my youngest, very properly looking to the future instead of wallowing in the past.

We bought cheese, croissants and fruit for the journey, then boarded the overnight train. There were no frills. The compartment was old fashioned and uncomfortable; there was no dining car, buffet or tea trolley, and the loos were – well – French. Although it was an overnight journey, there was no provision for getting comfortable, just thinly upholstered upright seats. The only other occupant was an Englishman, who looked as if he would have preferred to travel first class, had it been possible. He greeted our entrance with a curt nod.

We set off, and I watched the flat countryside sliding by, interspersed with familiarly named stations: Amiens, Reims, Dijon, Lyons, Grenoble. I thought how deadly the journey would have been by road, and felt that the enormous fare of £90 had been well worth it. Veronica was already asleep, and the Englishman was gently snoring. Hadn't his wife ever told him about the habit, if he had a wife, of course? Maybe men of his class don't marry and procreate. In which case, how did they manage to corner all the top jobs? I continued to gaze through the window, sitting upright on the hard seat, but my head began to nod and, although I jerked it several times into wakefulness, I must have gone to sleep eventually, because I woke to see Veronica ravenously demolishing the croissants.

"Hey, leave some for me!"

Veronica looked hurt.

"Of course I will," she said, between mouthfuls. "I thought you'd never wake up."

The Englishman smiled indulgently and took a swig from his hip flask.

"Nearly there," he said.

A few more hundred miles together and he would have completely thawed out.

I knew that we were in Italy, when the station signs began to have Zs in them, sometimes even double Zs, but the great joy was when we saw a name spelled out against the ornate ironwork of the final station: BOLOGNA. Good old French railways. Mission accomplished. My Mini and the Englishman's MG were on the top layer of the transporter, and a very steep ramp with narrow guides for the tyres was the only way down. It looked terrifying, and even the Englishman seemed uneasy. In Boulogne, our cars had been driven up for us by a railway employee, but they would not be driven down again for us, not here. Most of the Italian workers were Communists, the heirs of Garibaldi, and they were not going to ease the paths of the foreign bourgeoisie. The Englishman went first. He swallowed hard, squared his shoulders, looked straight ahead and guided his car to the ground. I clapped to congratulate him, he nodded for the second time that day, and drove off.

"To his villa in Tuscany I suppose," I said aloud.

"Come off it, Mum," said Veronica. "We are doing just the same as him, only he's got more style with it."

Stung into action by my ungrateful progeny, I climbed up and sat rigidly in the driving seat. As I grasped the wheel, my hands felt sweaty, and I looked down at Veronica, who was standing far below, getting ready to guide me.

"Left a bit; now right, now left. LEFT, I SAID. You're going too fast. Mind that girder!"

I made it without crashing, and the car landed safely on Italian *terra firma*. True, the baggage had lurched sideways, but it was still intact, and the car looked refreshed after twenty-four hours of inactivity, unlike us. We both needed a good wash. I looked around at the bare goods yard and the railway workers in their blue overalls, and wondered what should be our next step. Veronica did what she always did in times of crisis, unpinned her long hair and began to brush out the tangles, and it was soon a yard-long swathe of gold, rippling in the sunshine. Of course, she was ogled at by the Bolognese workers, and that was her intention. She's no slouch, my daughter! Of course it paid off. A guard introduced us to a nearby hotel, where the proprietors let us use their bathroom and toilet. Refreshed, we stepped out into the town.

"I'm hungry," said Veronica, "and we're in Italy, so we must have a pizza."

We bought a couple from a baker's shop, but she was disappointed and complained, "No better than Sainsbury's."

I tartly explained that there was nothing much you could do with a ring of dough and a few ingredients stuck on top, even though the olives were probably local. I was still smarting from the allusion to my lack of style. On her part, Veronica had lost her faith in both Italy and her long-suffering mother, and wanted to get on to the next stage.

"If you know the way," she said aggressively.

I slammed in the clutch, concentrated on left-hand driving, and wondered if I had done my sums wrong. Perhaps, Veronica was still an adolescent.

Chapter 7

We set out for the port of Ancona, more than a hundred miles away, where I had already booked a ferry to Greece. Initially, I had difficulty leaving Bologna, going twice round a roundabout before hitting the main road, still rattled from the slight "spat" with Veronica. We travelled with no serious incident, except for the paucity of stopping places – comfort stations, as the Americans call them. Thirty miles on, I was bursting and had to do something about it. There were no hedges, so I pulled up the car in the shadow of an underpass. The traffic thundered ahead unheeding, but a lorry driver coming in the opposite direction leaned out, waved and said something in Italian. Brazenly, I waved back, still squatting, but Veronica shrank further down into the anonymity of the Mini, and remained tight-lipped for the rest of the journey. We passed a sign to Ravenna, the city which has the famous Byzantine mosaics. I was tempted to make a diversion, but I had booked a double cabin on the next ferry, and I didn't want to arrive late and lose my deposit. What is a measly deposit when compared with Byzantine mosaics, I asked myself, but the fact that I drove on made me suspect that I was getting old and stodgy.

We arrived at Ancona with an hour to spare, went directly to our cabin and stretched out on the bunks. The trouble with cabins is that they are usually just above the car deck, in the bowels of the ship, and very stuffy. This one was no exception. True, we had a porthole, which let in daylight, but, unfortunately no air, so we had a couple of hot, sweaty night to endure.

"We'd have been better up on deck with the backpackers," I said. "Cheaper, too."

"Oh, come on, mum," said Veronica, "you're too old. I'd be embarrassed."

I let that pass to avoid any more *angst*. However, she did allow us to spend the daytime up on the deck in the sunshine, gazing at the Adriatic. Then, the ferry swung into Corfu and our first Greek island. From then on, we were sailing in the Ionian sea, straining to catch our first glimpse of the Greek mainland at Patras. We watched the ferry navigate the mole and enter the harbour of this, the largest city on the Peloponnese. It is a sprawling complex of 100,000 people, topped by a medieval castle on the heights. Twenty years ago, my first sight of the place had been from a humble bus; now I was waiting to drive down the ramp of the ferry in my own car. There must be a significance here somewhere.

"Just means you're twenty years older," said Veronica. Not an ounce of romanticism in her, that one!

Of course, Veronica didn't know about Costas, and I had no intention of telling her. Where was he now? He would be twenty years older, too, and had probably developed the Greek male gut, just as I had developed the English female pear-shape. Ah, me, golden days! I remembered the visit to Delphi, and feeding a gypsy's monkey with grapes...

The car in front of me moved off the ramp, and I automatically put in the clutch and drove the Mini down on to the hard. All days can be golden, if only you look for them. Youth doesn't have the monopoly of wonder...

"Look out!" said my youngest. "They're waving you to stop."

I snapped out of my reverie as a large uniformed Greek

with wide shoulders advanced menacingly and peered through the window into the back of the poor, overloaded Mini. Something seemed to excite him, and I turned to look at what it was. Somewhere along the journey, the cardboard box containing my Amstrad Computer had slipped out of the covering of towels and blankets in which it was packed, and one corner jutted out. The sharp-eyed Greek had spotted it and, in voluble Demotic, demanded an explanation. Even the rudiments of the language now left me, and all I could do was mime the use of a keyboard and mutter,

"Typewriter. Typewriter."

He didn't understand, and beckoned to a more senior colleague. They looked in bemusement as I stabbed my knee like a maniac.

"Typewriter, typewriter!"

By now, a queue had formed behind the car, and angry motorists were leaning out of the windows. A truck driver, who had got into the wrong stream, was even brandishing a spanner, whether at me, or the police, I couldn't tell. Tempers were rising; would they impound the computer? Then, Veronica's hair suddenly became unpinned, and the police looked at each other. The senior customs official sighed and peremptorily waved us on, with a gesture which probably meant Greek for "get lost". As I drove off, I saw the junior officer turn away in disgust. Why did they let us go? Was it the log jam, or my frenzy, or Veronica's insecure hairpins? Veronica was sure that it was the latter, and used it as a scoring point for the rest of the journey.

Free of the harbour, we set off on the road to Nafplion, 70 miles away. According to the map, the route was mostly motorway, so with luck, we should do it in a couple of hours. The first stretch hugged the coast, and we could see across the Gulf of Corinth to where Delphi loomed above, with

Parnassos as a backdrop. Again, I remembered Costas, and how we had wandered around the site. There were very few tourists in those days, and we were able to scramble over the ancient stones without any barriers to hinder us.

"It's getting hot," said Veronica. "How much further is it?"

"We'll be on the motorway soon. Look, there's the tollgate."

I paid the toll fee, and bought a tray of peaches from a Greek god with melting eyes and patched trousers.

"*Efcharisto*," I said.

Soon, we were spinning along at 70mph and eating peaches, oblivious to the juice, which dribbled from our mouths and down our clothes. The approaching end to our journey gave us an exhilaration that verged on drunkenness. I felt like singing or weaving in and out across the road, but I did neither. We skirted New Corinth, which didn't look too bad as we came at it from the different approach. We raced through Argos. There would be time enough to explore it later. The Mini bumped over the railway lines outside Argos, and we came onto the straight road lined with eucalyptus trees, and there, pointing skyward, was the familiar outline of Palamidi. I nosed my way impatiently through Nafplion, past Syntagma Square, past the bobbing boats, past the post office, and past the barracks. We went through Gregory's village, came onto the sandy track with coloured bee-hives on the left and a monastic building on the right, then drove down and round a series of bends, winding through the orange groves, until we came to point where I knew that the house would be revealed. I took a deep breath as I swung out of the bend, and there it was.

"Wow!" said Veronica.

It stood white and gleaming, surrounded by a fringe of olive trees. As we drew nearer we were able to see the details of the house. A roof made of traditional terracotta tiles sloped down to form a cool veranda; white walls gleamed pristine against the background of greenery; windows reflected the late morning sun, which shone straight across from the Argolian plain. We went into the gateless drive, and bumped along past the builders' rubble, coming to a halt near the kitchen door. We climbed from the car, carefully stretching out the limbs that had sustained us for over 2,000 miles, and I looked at my territory. Dear old Gregory had been right all along. I was the owner of a villa that had cost the same price as a poky flat in Tolon. I surveyed the hamlet of Profitis Illias, and realised for the first time that, at its edge, and towering above the cluster of small buildings, there was a Byzantine church. It was the church of the Prophet Elijah, spreading over us like a benediction. Meanwhile, Veronica was on a cursory tour of inspection. She ran her fingers along the smooth white walls.

"Is it really made of concrete?"

"Yes, but it doesn't look like it, does it? It's more like marble."

We started heaving boxes out of the car, but then a movement in the grass caught Veronica's eye. A large tortoise crossed in front of us and solemnly walked from one side of the garden to the other before disappearing in the undergrowth. A tiny cloud passed in front of the sun as he did so. Was this another portent, like the black sails? The only tortoise myth I knew about was the one which dropped from an eagle's beak and killed Aeschylus. Nasty, certainly, but surely nothing to do with our present *testudo*. I felt uneasy, but dismissed any speculation as fanciful, and was cross with Veronica because, if she hadn't been standing around gawping, neither of us would have seen it. I hoped that she would be an asset in the coming weeks as we settled in. Otherwise, I would have been better advised to fill up the passenger seat with luggage. When we finished unpacking, I was able to view the large living room. Even with the stripped pine lining, it looked bare.

"You'll have to get some furniture," said Veronica. "Maybe that estate man will help. Let's face it, your Greek is hardly up to shopping standard."

I was about to retort when I heard a vehicle crunch across the gravel. Gregory unfolded his long legs from the Volvo and came towards us, beaming.

"You like?" he said." You like?"

Chapter 8

Settling In

Next morning, I awoke to brilliant sunshine, and slowly levered myself up from the floor. The previous night, we had spread rugs on the tiles, and with rolled up towels as pillows, had gone to sleep. I looked across to Veronica, who was still asleep on her improvised bed, and dimly remembered that Gregory had called, but I wasn't too certain what else had happened. The last lap of the journey and our arrival had been so confused that I wondered if I had dreamt his visit. I carefully stepped over Veronica and went out on to the veranda. The view was all that I had dreamed of: the plain of Argos and the distant hills, behind which nestled Agamemnon's Mycenaean palace. Nearer to hand, I looked around at my half acre of rough ground, which I hoped one day to turn into a garden. Even in its wild state, it gave off an intoxicating scent of thyme and other herbs whose names I didn't even know in English, let alone in Greek. I stood on the veranda in the sunshine, the warmth enveloping me like a mantle, although the sun hadn't yet freed itself from the reluctant horizon. I stood there, soaking up the scene that I had visualised so often back home in Wales, when a movement in the lane leading to the hamlet made me turn. I saw an elderly peasant woman herding half a

dozen goats, guiding them with a gnarled olive stick. She had
on a black headscarf and was wearing a black skirt that came
down below her knees. She had daps on her feet and black
three-quarter socks, but they didn't meet her skirt, and so there
was revealed a skittish glimpse of bare peasant leg. On an
impulse, I waved to her and, after a moment's hesitation, she
waved back. I had made my first contact with my Greek
neighbours.

While I was relishing this event, I heard a few thumps
coming from the house, and soon a bleary eyed Veronica
emerged, her nakedness wrapped in a blanket. She squinted at
the scene before her: the green of the olive trees and the
lighter green of the orange plantations, and beyond them, the
plain of Argos with the morning mist rapidly evaporating. My
daughter is rarely at a loss for words, but this time she was half
asleep, and as she breathed in the herb-laden air, she uttered
the only expression that came to her.

"Wow" she said for the second time in the last twenty-four
hours, and dropped the blanket.

My daughter is young and healthy, however, and that brief
utterance of wonder as she picked up the discarded blanket
soon turned to the practicalities of life.

"What's for breakfast?"

I crossed to the sink area and filled the electric kettle, which
had rattled all the way from Wales, then we sat down on the
steps outside, to drink tea and eat crumbled biscuits.

The house consisted of two bedrooms, a tiled bathroom and
one large, all-purpose living area with a sink, a fridge, and a
central fireplace with a chimney that went straight up to the
roof. All the rooms were lined with tongued and grooved
wood in a warm honey colour, and I was glad that I had spent
the extra money and arranged for Gregory to fix it. As we
finished our makeshift meal, I resolved to go to Nafplion to

stock up with provisions. There was a small shop in the village of Agios Nicolias, and it was within walking distance, but I decided to buy the initial big purchases in the town. The added advantage to going to Nafplion was that Gregory's office was there and I could consult him about buying furniture.

Veronica's truculent advice still rankled but I had to admit that she was right about the paucity of my language, and I certainly needed assistance in buying expensive items such as furniture.

At the office Gregory was instantly helpful. "My father will take you to some friends of mine who have a furniture shop," he said. "How about tomorrow?"

Was it professional care for a client, or was it the salesman prompting him? I reserved judgement.

Early the following morning, Gregory dropped off his father at my house. Pappa Yannis had come straight from the church which towered above us, the church of the Prophet, and he was in full ecclesiastical gear. Had it been a liturgy, or had he been hearing confessions? What counted as a sin in the small hamlet of Profitis Illias? Blasphemy, skipping devotions, stealing? Or did they aspire to more interesting transgressions such as incest, adultery or murder? I couldn't tell from the priest's expression, because whatever had been going on up there in the church, he still looked as innocent and cherubic as ever, and pointedly diverted his gaze from Veronica, who was stretched out on the veranda, sunbathing. There was a problem when he got into my car; his heavy chain with a gold cross got caught in the unaccustomed right-hand steering wheel, but I managed to unwind him, and we drove off, Pappa Yannis sitting in the front passenger seat while I acted as chauffeur.

We came to a major road with the sea on one side and a few factories on the other. Some were functioning, some had obviously given up, and others were still in the half-built stage and looked as if they were going to stay that way. This was Nafplion's attempt at an industrial complex, but it had ground to a halt, whether from incompetence or lack of interest, I couldn't tell. The desolation was accentuated by a large gypsy camp nearby, with lean dogs and ravenous goats, which followed us with hungry eyes as we drove past the fenced enclosure. The *epipla* (furniture shop) was a stylish, modern emporium set in this wasteland. It had two large windows displaying bedroom furniture, but they looked incongruous in that bleak stretch of stunted sea-grass. A flag flew bravely from the roof, promoting an industrial centre that had long ceased to be viable.

I learned later that Nafplion was fated to suffer from near-misses. After the War of Independence, the first Greek Parliament was set up in Syntagma Square, and for a brief period, Nafplion was the country's most important town, but only a year later, the Parliament moved to Athens, which then became the official capital, and Nafplion's glory faded. The same thing happened to the railway. It had extended from Argos to the city centre, but it was now disused, only the empty station and ticket hall served as a reminder of what it had been. Again, at my arrival, I noticed that the town was plastered with posters heralding Nafplion's selection as the next European City of Culture. The workmen were already beginning to smarten up the town, laying patterned cobbles round the parks, but alas, before I left for good, the cherished cultural crown had been transferred to Salonika.

But back to the *epipla*. As we drew nearer to the shop, I was full of misgivings, sensing that I would be eclipsed by Pappa Yannis. Already, his aura had overwhelmed me and my poor little hatchback. What if he insisted on choosing the furniture for me? What if it was wildly expensive, and what if I didn't like it? My imperfect Greek couldn't convey anything as subtle as: "It isn't what I had in mind." How would he take a blunt *Ochi* (no)? Is it permitted to argue with the Church, especially when it is dressed in full regalia? I pulled up outside the shop with some trepidation, but my worries were needless. The shopkeeper stood at the entrance and greeted the priest, kissing his hand, then he turned to me and said in excellent English,

"Good morning, madam. I believe you are interested in purchasing some furniture."

We went round the showroom and I chose two single beds, a table and chairs, and a desk for the computer, all in honey-coloured pine, and, as an afterthought, a rather spartan sofa. The shopkeeper promised delivery by the following day, and I paid him with the last of my crisp new notes from the bank. From now on, I would be dealing with the local currency, which is still legal but incredibly tattered and stained. It seemed as if there was a finite number of bank notes in Nafplion, which went round and round and were never renewed. Mr. Epipla took the money, and he and Pappa Yannis disappeared into a back office, talking softly together, while I inspected my new purchases. When they emerged, Pappa Yannis looked more cherubic than ever, but whether it was due to commission on the transaction, or an on-the-spot absolution, I had no means of knowing. As we went out, we passed a young man, who was sitting on the pavement and leaning against the struts of the shop window. He looked bedraggled and was obviously stoned out of his mind. Was he a Greek hippy? Where had he got the dope? Was it endemic, even here, and had I brought Veronica from one frying pan into a Greek fire?

"Bulgarian!" said Pappa Yannis, pulling aside his skirt, his face distorted and angry.

For one awful moment, I thought he was going to give the lad a kick, but he contained himself and went to the car.

Bulgar, vulgar, is that where the adjective came from? A little shaken by witnessing this other side to the kindly priest, I drove back along the same road, passing the gipsy encampment again. They'd been doing the weekly wash, and the wire fence was covered with bright clothing drying in the sun, but with my new insight into the character of the priest, I wondered what his reaction was going to be. I never found out because I was coming to a bend and had to concentrate on going round it left-handed, but I sensed rather than saw what I took to be a contemptuous drawing aside of the long black skirt that had been concealing nylon socks and scuffed shoes.

Chapter 9

Getting Organised

The furniture came; the water board came and installed a meter; and Dimitri came. He was another of Gregory's buddies but more of the age of Pappa Yannis, and his job was to put a fence round my property. "To keep out the sheep and the goats."

Dimitri was sixtyish with a weather-beaten face, and he proudly explained, in a mixture of Greek and English, that he had fought with the British to save Athens from the Communists after WW2. I was hardly in a position to enter into a political argument, especially as he had brought me a large bunch of grapes, but I wasn't amused. In 1944, many of us on the Left were furious with the British Government for interfering in Greece. Throughout the war years, the Communists under Markos Vaphiades had fought bravely against the Germans and had freed three quarters of the country. Why shouldn't they have the right to enter Athens! We didn't know until later that a pact had been made with Stalin at Yalta, whereby he was to have the Balkans, and the Allies would have Greece. It's a matter of history now, but the memories were still bitter. I gave Dimitri a cup of tea, which he may or may not have appreciated, but he certainly appreciated Veronica, sitting in a bikini and reading a book. Was she ever going to do anything, apart from sitting around half naked?! When he had gone, I realised with surprise that, instead of reading a magazine, as I thought, she was studying my sale-of-house contract, which had been translated into English.

"It says here," she said, pointing with her finger. "It says here that he undertakes to plant some lemon and olive trees."

The girl was getting useful after all!

"Where are the trees you promised me?" I asked Gregory the next day.

He gave me a reproachful look. I had never questioned him before, but he came with his father a few days later, trees trailing out of the boot of his Volvo. Pappa Yannis, with his skirts hitched up, dug some holes around the edge of my property, and Gregory manhandled the trees into them. As they worked, the priest looked more like one of his militant brethren in Kazantzakis' book (*The Fratricides*) than the solemn patriarch I had got used to. I was puzzled and the doubts began to creep in again. I couldn't tally this homespun episode with the brand new office in the town and the fax machine. What was the scale of Gregory's agency, or was it a front for something more sinister? Perhaps it was an elaborate trap to ensnare naive foreigners. I looked round at my house and my plot, and had to admit that, so far, Gregory had played fair. I wrenched my mind away from unkind thoughts and struggled to and fro, carrying sloshing water buckets, as I helped with the watering.

Halfway between Nafplion and the town of Argos there was a large general store, which sold every sort of household necessity, and the prices were modest. I drove there to supplement the gaps in my domestic set-up: mugs, tea towels, a toilet seat, a trolley to wheel out on to the veranda, scouring pads, etc. No teapot was to be had. Greeks rarely drink tea, but with the stuff I had brought in the Mini, the furniture from the *epipla*, and these added purchases, I was beginning slowly to turn the anonymous rooms into something approaching a home. I placed the computer desk so that I could look out across the Argos plain as I worked; the meagrely padded sofa faced the fireplace; the dining table and chairs were positioned to catch the morning sun; and the blue rugs donated by my middle daughter, Penny, broke up the rather prosaic plastic floor tiles. There was no need for curtains because the windows were fitted with slatted wooden shutters.

This essay in furniture arrangement and soft furnishing was great fun but, as the days sped by, I was beginning to be conscience-stricken about Veronica. She could be exasperating but she was my daughter after all, and she had given up her vacation to accompany me to Greece. So far, she hadn't had much of a holiday, obsessed as I had been with getting the house straight.

"Would you like to go for a walk?" I suggested one balmy afternoon.

"If you like."

"How about climbing up to the church?"

We walked through the silent hamlet, it was siesta time, and climbed up the steep path to the church. Unfortunately, it was locked, the Prophet was not at home. We consoled ourselves by looking out at the stunning view, which from that height revealed the waters of the Argonic Gulf, and I imagined Agamemnon and his fleet sailing southward. There was a thick rope that extended from the tower above us to where we were standing in the porch.

"What's this?" asked Veronica, playfully setting it swinging.

We looked up and saw that it was attached to an enormous

bell, which was housed in the tower, the rope being tantalisingly accessible. I looked at Veronica and Veronica looked at me, and for an instant our two generations combined and teetered on the edge of devilry.

"Dare we?"

I peered at the tiny houses far below and wondered what would happen if we pulled the rope and the bell clanged. Would the stick people inside run out in the street with memories of Germans and their atrocities, of Communists and their atrocities, or of Ottoman Turks with their even greater atrocities? We were sorely tempted, but only the thought of being hounded off the Peloponnese for lèse-majesté with regard to the Prophet Elijah prevented us. We walked back down the hill and had a sun-downer on the veranda instead. The outcome of the adventure was that it whetted Veronica's appetite for exploration. Next day, she decided to mooch off on her own and climb through the grove of old olive trees, to a cluster of rocks that were on the other side of the village and marked the highest point in the area. I had already noticed them and realised that they were much bigger than the small outcrops which littered the hill. They must have been hauled up there and were probably the remains of an old house, although, in Greece, the term "old" means more than the usual connotation. Maybe those unassuming building slabs had been there for more than two thousand years, or was I being fanciful? Veronica, who is very good with a camera, took a panoramic view from the top. The trick is to take a series of photographs so that each successive one is exactly fitted on to the one before. It requires steady hands, and Veronica's prints usually turned out to be spot on.

"You can see for miles," she said when she came down. "Almost to that other town; what's its name?"

"Argos."

"That's right, Argos. But it's a real scramble to get to the top. The boulders are so big, I could hardly clamber over them. And there were a couple of arches…"

"Arches?" I interposed.

"Yes, arches, oh, and some paving stones. I know you're mad on ruins, mum, but I don't think you should try and clamber up there. Let's face it, you're not as young as you were."

Dear, sweet, youngest. The epitome of "put down"!

Next time I was in Nafplion, I asked Gregory about the ruins. He stopped biting into a chocolate bar and paused in one of his import/export fantasies, shipping marble or oranges to Russia, or something of that sort.

"Oh, that place," he said casually. "It was a staging post on the way to Epidavros."

EPIDAVROS! The most famous of the Greek amphitheatres, where Sophocles' *Antigone* was first performed, and *The Clouds* of Aristophanes, and many more plays, some of which have been lost forever. Epidavros was only twenty-five miles away from my place as the crow flies, and I imagined the ancient Greeks trekking on foot from the west, from Kalamata and Sparta. They would have realised that this was their last stop before reaching their goal. Some would have screwed up their eyes, searching for the first sight of Epidavros, but they would have been disappointed because, even from the high point that Veronica had reached, the amphitheatre would have been out of sight round the next headland. Maybe they swallowed their disappointment and sat down and rested for their last tea-break, herb tea, of course, and Arcadian honey. Perhaps some wandered down the hill and sat and chatted on the very patch that I had only that morning marked out for a paved courtyard. I felt very near to them, as near as one can be to anyone, over a gap of several thousand years.

"A staging post," Gregory had said casually, biting into a Mars bar.

Again, I was amazed at the way the Greeks treat their fabulous past. To be fair, I suppose the butchery of recent wars is much more real to them, butchery that our island protected us from. Would we have such a sanguine attitude to the immediate past if we had actually been occupied by the Nazis? I remember a low point in WW2 and an early lover saying to me,

"If they come, you'll end up in a stud farm, and I'll be gibbering about in the Highlands."

I resolved to climb up and inspect the staging post, but not under the critical eye of my daughter. I would wait until Veronica had gone back to University.

Chapter 10

Epidavros

Veronica, after a slow start had now got the archaeology bug.

"What's that place, that theatre you were talking about?"

"Epidavros?"

"That's it, Epidavros. I've only got just over a week left; can we go there? It will be a talking point for me back at college."

I welcomed the interest she was showing, even though it was partly aimed at bragging to her peers. We set off early one Greek morning, blue sky, blue sea, tiny blue birds, blue cyclamen in the cracks between the rocks, and overall the heady scent of thyme and olives and ripening oranges. Epidavros is eight miles inland from the sea, rising from a fertile plain. It is more than just an amphitheatre; in ancient times it had been the Greek equivalent of a sanatorium, the dominant building being a temple to Aesculapius, the god of healing. Alongside were the remains of a two-storey building, which must have been a hospital where the sick could stay and wait to be cured.

"Just like Lourdes," said Veronica.

I realised with chagrin that many of the pilgrims I had romantically visualised back at my place as being the devotees of Dionysus, the god of wine and drama, were actually the followers of the more sober god Aesculapius. I'd have to adjust my perceptions slightly. Beyond the temple and overlooking the valley below, we came across a sizeable, oblong stadium with stone seats on either side of a running track, which was one *stade* (200 yds.) long. There was even a brass marker indicating the beginning of the course, and Veronica ran the whole length in 45 seconds.

"That will certainly be something to brag about," she said breathlessly.

For me, the high point of the visit was the amphitheatre, its semi-circular rows of stone seats towering upwards from the *skene* (stage). I thought of the thousands that had sat there and watched the plays, and were still doing so right up to the present time. For the priests of Aesculapius, attendance at the amphitheatre would have rounded off their patients' cure; a sprint along the running track followed by a dose of Sophocles, applying the dictum that a regenerated body needs a regenerated mind.

"It's huge," said Veronica. "Bigger than the Albert Hall."

I remembered that the Albert Hall had circular baffles hanging from the dome to help with its acoustics, but here there was no need for such a device, just a carefully chosen site in the open air, where a whisper from the *skene* could be heard as far as the back row. We saw a group of tourists experimenting with one of their number, who was standing far below, in the middle of the stage.

"Say something, buddy."

"What shall I say?"

"Say something in Greek."

"OK. Phi, Kappa, Delta".

The Greek of an American campus ritual rang out loud and clear.

We explored for several hours, and after coffee in a restaurant on the site, we set off for home, taking the coastal road and squinting into the setting sun.

"What are those white blocks of stone?" asked my youngest, pointing to where a deep gash had been gouged out of the hillside.

In a way, this was the most miraculous of all the sights of that day. We were passing marble quarries, which were still being mined, and had been so uninterruptedly since the age when Sophocles first set stylus to parchment.

Before Veronica leaves these pages and goes back to University, perhaps I should tell you a little more about her. She is very attractive, but very thin (scraggy, her sisters used to say), and her main ambition in life is to be a blues singer. Indeed, she has a good, smoky voice, rather like the late Peggy Lee, but on a bad day, more like a female Leonard Cohen. This singing ambition plays havoc with her academic studies and encourages her to behave outrageously. The flagship to this behaviour is her long blond hair, which reaches down to her knees. Sometimes, she coils it queen-like on top of her head, at others she lets it drop in a yard-long plait down her back, like a Tatar princess. When she wanted to overwhelm or intimidate the latest boyfriend, she wore it loose, in a cascade of gold, as she had done to the railway workers in Bologna. But in serious situations, in a magistrate's court after a drug bust, or when applying for a temporary job, she wore it pulled back from her classical face in a heavy bun. In spite of her idiosyncratic life style, I was very fond of her, and still felt somewhat guilty about how little I had done to entertain her in the past few weeks.

"What would you like to do most before you go home?" I asked her.

"The market," said Veronica. "Let's go to the market."

The Wednesday market was the event of the week in Nafplion. Stalls were set up along *Odos 25 Martou* (25th.March St.), which was lined on the one side by dusty pine trees and on the other by the terraces of Palamidi. The stalls began at the bus station and continued for several hundred yards, then went past the Esso garage to meander into smaller side streets and the fish market. I consulted Gregory.

"My mother will take you round," he said, patting my hand. "You might miss something."

I had met Magda once, in Gregory's office, a quietly spoken woman in black, and much younger than her priestly husband. Would she mind having two foreigners foisted on her?

"Of course not," said Gregory dismissively. "Come to my house tomorrow, about 7.30, and I will arrange for her to be waiting for you."

When we drove up to the Petroulakis house on the following day, I heard the church bell in the village strike the half hour, but Magda clearly wasn't waiting for us. In fact, she looked surprised and flustered. She recovered enough to sit us on the veranda and bring us some coffee, but clearly something was amiss. We could hear her talking to Gregory, who still seemed to be in bed, and her voice was pitched a little higher than normal. Had Gregory forgotten to tell her about the arrangement? We drank our coffee and eventually Magda came out, with her coat on and carrying a basket. She was now a little more composed, and we drove off to the town. Gregory would be following later. I parked the car by the harbour and we walked to Odos 25 Martou. The stalls were being erected in two parallel lines down the middle of the street, over the now defunct railway lines and the remains of the ticket office.

"What happened to the trains?" I asked Magda.

"Gone, all gone," she said, or something like that.

When, I wondered? Had the Greeks suffered the equivalent

of a Dr. Beeching, or had the unrealised hopes of being the country's Capital demoralised them? What a shame! I would have liked to chunter along the single track to Argos, past the eucalyptus trees, with the sea twinkling on the right hand side. Perhaps I should introduce the City Fathers to the idea of the little Welsh trains, which do so well in the tourist season back home. I was surprised to see that the market was sparsely attended, some stall holders only just beginning to set out their produce. However, during the hour or so that we were there many more people came, and soon it was as busy a place as I remembered it from my last brief visit. Supplementing the stall holders were the gypsy women, moving up and down the road, straight backed, swinging from the waist, with their full skirts, headscarves tinkling with coins. They were selling baskets, clothes pegs, charms, sad-eyed monkeys.

"Lucky charm for the lovely ladies?"

Neither I nor Magda fitted the bill but it was nice to be included along with Veronica. She bought some of the blue beads that are traditionally said to bring good luck to the wearer and ward off the evil eye, and I looked sideways at Magda. Would the priest's wife consider it blasphemy to subscribe to such beliefs? But Magda was gaily drinking in the bustle, the colours, the smells, and the vibrancy of Nafplion's Wednesday market. I had made a list of purchases I wanted to make, including fish for supper and I racked my brains for the Greek word for fish. "*Psaros?*" No, that meant grey. *Psevtia?* No, that meant "liar". It was certainly Ps – something, but what? Then I remembered and turned to Magda.

"*Pou einai to Psari?*" (Where is the fish)

Magda smiled, delighted at my minimal Greek, and pointed to the far end of the market, where the fish stalls were grouped. Lying on the slabs were malevolent monsters, which I certainly wouldn't have wished to encounter when they were alive. There were others, less frightening, in electric blues and vivid orange, whose names I didn't know; there were crabs and lobsters and shrimps, which I did recognise but they were bigger than any I had seen before. In front was a mini-octopus, its eyes open in death as it drooped over the edge of its marble slab. I remembered trying to eat octopus one day, in a restaurant in France, and finding that it tasted like rubber. Faced with such a variety, what should I choose for supper? Under Magda's guidance, I bought a cod-like creature that looked safely familiar.

"*Poli kala, poli kala,*" (Very good) said Magda, nodding in anticipation of my coming pleasure.

At another stall, Veronica bought an assortment of fresh herbs; thyme, rosemary, marjoram etc.

"They'll remind me of Greece," she said. Perhaps the visit hadn't been a failure after all.

We finished our shopping and walked on to Gregory's office, so that he could take his mother home. We were laden with fish, purple figs, potatoes, peaches and coriander, all crammed into bright blue plastic bags. As we crossed the square by the church of St. George, its bell rang out the hour.

"It only chimed nine times," said Veronica.

"Nonsense, it's ten o'clock."

"I'm sure it struck nine," she said, then she shrugged her shoulders dismissively . "Typical Greeks!"

I began to have an uneasy foreboding, and as soon as we met up with Gregory, I asked him the time.

"Just gone nine," he said.

And I felt my mouth open like the fish in my plastic bag. There was a pause and then Gregory suddenly punched his forehead.

"You didn't know! The clocks went back last night."

He turned to Magda and laughingly explained. I didn't

laugh. No wonder Magda was unprepared when we called. Why didn't he warn us? He should have realised that we wouldn't know, stuck out there in Profitis Ilias, and unable to understand the radio. I not only didn't laugh, I was furious, and put this down as one more item on the list I was mentally compiling against Gregory. We left the office, our dignity in shreds.

We had fish for supper that night and it was as good as Magda had promised, but the ignominy of the morning still rankled. However, I was determined not to let the incident spoil my daughter's final memories of Greece, and on the last evening, I took her for a farewell dinner at the restaurant by the sea. Again, I saw no black sails. The earlier portents must have been wrong, or maybe we were now under the protection of the Prophet Elijah. In Greek restaurants there are often groups of men dining without their women, another example of Mediterranean machismo, and this restaurant was no exception. As Veronica threaded her way to our table, quite a few male heads were turned in her direction, so why hadn't Gregory responded to her? During the whole six weeks, he had barely acknowledged her presence. Was he scared of me? Did I put him off? Or did he think that she would be in Greece for such a short time that she was not worth pursuing? To be charitable, maybe he was treating us as a Greek family and accepting the restrictions which applied to Greek men, which were designed to protect the virginity of unmarried Greek females. Poor Gregory, whatever his reasons Veronica would leave untouched by him, when, did he but know it, Veronica was very far from being a virgin. Poor lamb, Gregory I mean, not Veronica.

The morning of departure came and we set off, taking the main road to Corinth. At the isthmus, I went on to a secondary road, which hugged the sea all the way to Athens, passing tiny villages with pink houses. At intervals there were stalls set out on the beaches, where the owners grilled sardines over charcoal. We sat at one of the stalls and ate bread and sardines with our fingers, drank a local version of retzina, and looked out at the distant island of Salamis. We didn't talk very much; there seemed very little to say, soaked as each of us were with our own impressions of that final journey.

Athens airport is like any other international airport, and after the formalities were completed, I wished Veronica a safe journey, and she passed through the barrier as if she were just crossing to the other side of the road. As a family, we are not over sentimental, but I was reluctant to leave before I saw her plane taxiing on to the runway and taking off. Then, I turned and headed home. I took the same coastal road and drove along, drunk with the sea air, the lingering effect of the retzina, and a maudlin sense of loss at the thought of flesh of my flesh flying overhead and rapidly increasing the space between us. Dear youngest daughter, I hope the next few months will treat you well.

Chapter 11

An Unexpected Development

I missed my daughter, I even missed her abrasiveness, but now, back home, I was confronted by an item that had remained untouched since I had slipped it past the customs at Patras – the computer. It stood there on the new pine desk and glowered at me. I must explain that this was no casual acquisition of mine but a serious part of the whole Greek enterprise. True, I had come to the warm south to cosset my aging bones, but the principal motivation was to do some writing. It had been my hobby for most of my life, but nothing had come of it so far. There were always things that got in the way: marriage, children, jobs, divorces, ironing. Now, with retirement, and money to spare, I had set up this idyll where I could turn a hobby into something more tangible. I realised, as I watched the exhaust from Veronica's plane fog the runway, that the old excuses no longer applied and that with her departure I had reached crunch time.

I had already started to write my autobiography when I retired to Wales, a year earlier, and I had brought the first chapters to Greece with me, intending to continue with them. When I looked at the turgid prose now, I wasn't satisfied with it. It was boring and dull. My life had been neither; how, then, had I ended up with such nonsense? I resolved to start again from scratch, and where better to do it than in sunny Greece, looking out onto the plain of Argos. A writers' course I had once attended emphasised the importance of the initial sentences, both to open the eyes of a cynical publisher and, subsequently, to attract the average traveller at the average bookstall. The most riveting opening sentence in a modern novel that I had come across was in a work of Rose Macaulay:

"Take my camel, dear," said my aunt Dot, as she climbed down from this animal on her return from High Mass.

There was also Virgil, precise and to the point:

Of Arms and the Man I sing.

And who has bettered Dickens?

It was the best of times; it was the worst of times.

Dare I emulate these professionals? I was prepared to try, so I sat at the computer and began to type.

"My first memory was of coal trucks being passed along on cables, defining the ridges of the opposite mountain."

"Defining the ridges", that was good, very good, but who would be interested? The grim South Wales valleys are green again and the coal mines are dead, even though the antagonists, Scargill and Thatcher, are still alive. In order to catch the interest of the reading public, there has got to be a human dimension. How about this?

"The toddler pressed her chubby fingers against the window pane, smearing the glass and tracing the outline of the trucks on the skyline."

That was better, the image more tactile, and writing in the third person seemed to let the words flow more easily, but there was still the old trouble. How can you revitalise a long dead situation? Perhaps it could be spiced up. Perhaps the toddler could fall out of the window and tumble down twenty steps. There were twenty steps in my old home in Ogmore Vale, but I never fell down them. How much poetic licence is permissible? As I struggled with this moral dilemma, I heard a car draw up and, then, heard Gregory's voice.

"Can I come in?"

He was probably coming to look at the blocked drain, and I went out, spanner in hand, but, in fact, he'd come to invite me to supper.

"I thought you might be lonely," he said.

I was touched, and, several hours later, we were sitting at a table in a restaurant. It was not like the usual tourist restaurant, and seemed to be patronised by businessmen; indeed, Gregory nodded to several of them as we came in. It was tucked away in a back street, and had the atmosphere of an English club. The food was excellent and, moreover, it was hot. Chefs in the tourist cafés usually cook the chips and wait for them to coagulate while they prepare the rest of the food. In this place, the moussaka arrived steaming and the accompanying chips were golden and crisp, almost as good as the *sglodion* (chips) we have back in Wales. Gregory talked compulsively, more than he had ever done before, and as he tackled the meal, he fantasised about his plans for the future. As far as I could gather, he wanted to become an entrepreneur, exporting oranges, olives and marble. I had seen rusty Russian ships moored in the harbour, having brought in tons of potatoes. Did he have designs on the Russian trade? Not exactly, he was looking westward and up a bit.

"Do you have any contacts in England, Eva? Import and export people?

"Afraid not." Gregory looked downcast. I tried to be a little more helpful. "Try a Chamber of Trade somewhere. London or Birmingham."

But he was already off on another tack, something to do with grapes from Kalamata. He was restive and couldn't stop talking; he ate the food in front of him as if it were his last meal before – what? I had the impression that he was eating to cover up an overwhelming excitement. He suddenly paused between mouthfuls and asked for the umpteenth time,

"You like the house?"

"Yes I like," I said, also for the umpteenth time. Really, this was becoming a bit of a bore!

He wiped his face with the serviette and we rose from the table.

"Would you like a drive to Palamidi?"

I was impressed that he continued to be the kind host, in spite of my deficiency on the entrepreneurial front.

"Yes, that would be nice," I replied, ever the dutiful guest.

As we left and as he fumbled over paying the bill, he still showed some uneasiness. Perhaps he was embarrassed that I was the only woman diner. That was it! The whole outing had been out of kilter, as far as Greek society was concerned; the businessmen's restaurant, the discussion with a woman about trading. He had tried to flatter me by treating me like a man, but, in the end, he wasn't quite brave enough. We drove up to Palamidi and stood on the ramparts of that Venetian pile, the lights of the town winking below in the darkness. Above, the disdainful stars dotted the sky and were reflected in the still waters, which softly lapped the island fortress of Boutzy, way out in the Argonic Gulf.

"Beautiful," I said.

Gregory was quiet as we stood there, and I was quiet too, storing the scene in my memory, to bring out on the bad days. Bad days would surely come; it's a denial of living, to pretend that life is eternal bliss. Then, Gregory broke the silence and gave an apologetic cough. As I turned to him he said with a rush,

"Would you like to make love?" Had I heard right!
"Please!" He was pleading like a schoolboy.

I was so totally unprepared for this development that, before
I could think of a crushing reply, I blurted out the truth.

"I haven't been with a man for years!"

"Does it matter?" He was speaking urgently now.

How could I tell him that it didn't matter either way,
because I was quite indifferent to sex and to him? Something
that was obviously of great importance in his life would be no
more than a trivial coupling in mine. His eyes were pleading,
desperate. A nearby VW Beetle bounced up and down
rhythmically, and I realised that Gregory had brought me to a
well known trysting place.

"Please," he said again.

Oh well, I thought, I suppose there's no harm in it, and the
setting is certainly romantic. We made love in the back seat of
the Volvo, and it was cramped and uncomfortable. Moreover,
the experience was physically painful. When it was over, we
clambered awkwardly out of the car to stretch our legs, and
stood again on the ramparts.

"Well?" he asked.

My god, was he expecting to be congratulated?

"It hurt," I told him.

He gave a typical Mediterranean shrug,

"That's just normal," he said.

How dare he, how dare this babe, who may even have been
a virgin, make pronouncements about my anatomy! I was
about to reply angrily, when I realised with a shock that he was
shivering. I looked at his hands, which were clutching the
balustrade, and the knuckles were white. The man was
terrified, and suddenly my anger turned to pity. Wordlessly, we
got back into the car and he drove me home. As we passed
through his village of Agios Nicholias, he turned to me and
said intensely,

"No one must know. You mustn't tell anyone."

He was still shaking. Why had he done it, why had he risked going against the grain of Society, his Church, and his Family? Back at the house and alone, I was inclined to laugh at myself. You're too old for this, my girl. Then I remembered the moment of penetration, and the pain as my body resisted the sudden onslaught. Next time, of course, it would be easier, but I had no intention of there being a next time.

Chapter 12

The Aftermath

I was in a quandary. I couldn't avoid future contact with
Gregory because he was central to my life in Greece. I
depended on him for help to deal with the bureaucracy relating
to the house, and for money matters generally. He also had this
pool of "buddies" he could call upon, from plumbers to
electricians, to gardeners. Was I prepared to ditch all this
because of a quick tumble on Palamidi? My own feeling
towards the episode was one of embarrassment, and I was
inclined to pretend that it had never happened, but what about
Gregory? His reactions had been so intense, particularly after
the event, that I couldn't believe that he would forget about it
entirely.

I was due to have tea with Magda on the following Sunday,
and I walked over to the Petroulakis house with a certain
amount of trepidation because I felt guilty about Gregory.
Since the mix-up at the Wednesday market, I had often
dropped in for a cool drink after visiting the local bakery, and I
had become very fond of Magda; we were even able to
communicate in a fractured way. We would sit out on her
veranda and look through the tendrils of vine leaves to the
roofs of Nafplion, far below, and drink orange juice. The
pitted oilcloth on the wooden table, the delicate smell of

tobacco flowers, the brilliant red of the geraniums, and at least eight skinny cats rampaging through their jungle of leaves and stems, seemed far away from Gregory and his up-to-date office. She seemed to enjoy my company, and was more relaxed with me than in the company of her go-getter son and her saintly husband. This particular Sunday, Gregory and a couple of cousins were also there, and the afternoon passed pleasantly enough, especially without the dominant presence of Pappa Yannis, who was attending a Mass in Nafplion. Gregory was a charming co-host, and not by a flicker of an eyelid did he let on that we had been less than discreet a few nights previously. I went home satisfied that the matter was now resolved and that our relationship could carry on as before. But not a bit of it! That same evening, Gregory came over, bringing a bottle of wine and obviously ready to carry on from where we had left off on the slopes of Palamidi. Either I had underestimated my sex appeal, or he was desperate.

I had to be honest to myself and admit that I was flattered by his persistence, and, with the excuse that it would be unkind to rebuff him, we made love again. A pattern began to emerge over the next few weeks. At odd times, in my house or on a quiet beach, or in an empty house belonging to his father, we made Shakespeare's "beast with two backs". Those were the days when the term 'toy boy' had not been invented, but we would certainly have qualified; a sixty year old matron and her twenty-six-year-old lover. This was not the kind of integration with the locals that I had envisaged when I was planning my Greek adventure, but I had to admit that it had its positive side; it was a human contact in an alien country and it was not altogether unpleasant. Was I kidding myself, was I less aloof than I believed myself to be, and was I succumbing to the charms of this Greek Lothario?

I continued to visit Magda, in spite of my liaison with her

son, and this was prompted by the fact that I was worried about her. She was always working, sometimes stumbling through tiredness, and the rest of the family seemed to take her for granted. The Petroukis house had many rooms, all cluttered with pictures and ornaments and effigies of the Virgin Mary. They reminded me of those nineteenth century Victorian furnishings in Britain, which were notorious for being time-consuming dust-traps. In addition, there were mountains of ironing. Greek men insist on a freshly laundered shirt each day and Gregory and his father were no exception. There was the garden, with flowers and vegetables to be tended; and beyond the house, approached through a small gate, was a sizeable field, where Magda grew oranges and olives and gathered wood. I had often seen her coming through that gate, her arms weighed down with branches that she had picked up to use on the open fire in the living room. But it was not only sympathy for an overburdened female that drew me to Magda; in some way, I felt that we were similar and shared a common bond, and it was more than gender; it was an indefinable something that I hadn't yet been able to understand.

One morning, sitting on the balcony and listening to Magda making us some coffee in the kitchen, I leaned back against the uprights and listened to the sounds coming up from the village. I heard the revving up of the three-wheeled bikes, with their rickety superstructure, that the farmers use to go to market, or to transport their families; then, the slap, slap of the women's daps as they collected bread from the bakery, or took dishes to be cooked in the communal oven. They were black clad women, of course, because the Greek mourning period is so long that, before one commemorative ceremony is over, another one begins. I heard the slosh of buckets of water being thrown down into the central drain, and the high-pitched voice of a mother scolding a child, and I imagined groups of gossiping women standing in doorways, as I had seen them do so often, when I was driving through on my way to Nafplion, black clad crones, like the Eumenides of old.

A sudden thought hit me: THE CRONES NEVER CAME TO MAGDA'S HOUSE. That was the bond that she and I shared: we were both isolated. I, because I was a foreigner; she, because she was the wife of a priest. For me, it was a cultural gap that I hoped one day would be closed, but for Magda, it was deep in the local hierarchy. Her position as a priest's wife removed her from any normal contact with the village people; she suffered the odium of the cleric without any of its benefits. I realised with a shock that, by association, a little of this had rubbed off on me, too. Along with Pappa Yannis, and Magda and Gregory, and to a lesser extent myself, we were tainted by thousands of years of the dread of the supernatural, which was inherent in the teaching of the church. The only one of us robust enough to ignore it, or to even thrive on it, was the venerable father of the village, with his gleaming gold cross and acute twinkling eyes.

I thought a great deal about Magda during the following days. She was lonely, but the men of her family were not aware of it, either that, or they didn't care. Magda spent her life as a drudge, and this incensed me. I particularly disliked Gregory's lordly attitude to his mother. One day, I came upon her washing his Volvo, and I was furious.

"How dare you let your mother wash your car?"

He was genuinely puzzled. "But she likes to do it."

That settled it. My tolerance of his playboy antics turned to dislike and I refused to let him touch me ever again. After an awkward cooling off period, we reverted to the earlier relationship of agent and client, and never referred to those brief weeks of madness, and, indeed, I think that in some ways Gregory was relieved to have got out of it so lightly. But why had he started in the first place and why had he continued to persist, when it obviously caused him so much stress? What made him gamble with what he had been trained to believe was the fate of his immortal soul?

The full extent of that gamble was only evident to me some time later, when the affair was over. I had bought some bread in Gregory's village and was starting to walk home, when I saw Pappa Yannis coming out of the small local church. He deliberately crossed the road to meet me, holding out his hand.

"*Kalimera, Kiria,*" he said.

I shook the hand with whatever reverence I could muster, "*Kalimera, Pappa.*"

He held my hand for just a fraction longer than I expected, and it gave me the opportunity to study that cherubic face. I remembered the hippy boy outside the furniture shop, and the edging away from any contact with the gypsies, and I felt impelled to look upward into the priest's eyes. Gazing at them, I realised with a shock that, beneath the surface calm, they were steely, with a touch of fanaticism. I thought back to that night on Palamidi. No wonder, Gregory had been terrified after his act of defiance. Pappa Yannis held all the cards: God, the Virgin, the Prophets, dark caverns of past religions, ancient magic, and, to cap it all, his sacred right as a father. The rebellion didn't have a chance, and if I hadn't ended it, no doubt Pappa Yannis would have found out and stopped it. Perhaps he already knew, and that was the reason for this morning's overture! He gave me a secret smile and said in carefully rehearsed English,

"I – am – glad – to – know – you."

This called for congratulations.

"Thank you," I said. "*Poli kala* (very good), you spoke well."

The steely eyes twinkled.

As I walked home with the crusty loaf of bread, I pondered over our encounter. I'd rumbled the wily priest, and now I understood the source of Gregory's terror, but that didn't explain why he had continued in his defiance for so many weeks. There was the testosterone, of course, which manifested itself in the way he gobbled his food and scoffed chocolate bars, but it had to be more than that. What was the great obsession which drove him on? Musing on the problem, I followed the road home as it wound upward, passing the brightly coloured bee-hives dotted on the hillside, and descending in a series of familiar bends until it reached the last one, where my house was revealed. It stood there in the bright sunshine, glistening white, the church of the prophet with its crenulated dome looming behind it, and beyond, the layer of purple hills. I remembered Veronica's first reaction,

"Wow!" she had said.

That was it, the house! Gregory lived at home, cosseted by his mother. His office in the town was rented, and so, unlike most of his business friends, he owned not a brick that he could call his own. But with my house, he had found the plot and developed it; he had overseen every wheelbarrow of cement, every tile, every stick of wood; he had chosen every window, every door handle, and every little extra feature, even the couple of steps up to the veranda. He was the patron of the whole gleaming edifice, and I was a secondary player, rather like the obligatory female in Mr. Manolis' brochures back in Paddington. But, secondary or not, he needed me; moreover, he needed my money. I'm not saying that the sexual overtures hid any ulterior motive, but they were certainly a try-on, and even when they failed, my value as owner of "his" house continued, and he made sure that we maintained a reasonable relationship.

"You like? You like?" now took on a deeper meaning. In Gregory-speak, it meant, "Do you like my house that I have built for you?"

Chapter 13

A Barren Piece of Land

There was no question about it. I owned the house and would do so until such a time as I decided to sell, if indeed that ever became necessary. Gregory could assume proprietorship in his head, but that would be meaningless in law, and his only avenue to satisfaction was vicarious possession through me. Was I dreaming all this? Had my brain been addled by the Greek sun? I tried to free myself from these fantasies. All that had happened, I told myself, was that I had bought a house with the help of a local agent, and it was now up to me to turn my new house into a home. I set about it accordingly.

The rooms were more or less furnished; it required just one more visit to the emporium on the way to Argos, to buy a trolley to wheel out on to the veranda, and a more substantial toilet seat, and I was complete. I turned my attention to the garden. I had a vision of vines twisting round the uprights of the veranda; a rockery with cyclamen and anemones and purple violas, all of which grow to twice the size of British ones; beds of lavender and poinsettia; some of Magda's sweet smelling tobacco flowers; and, perhaps, even a small fountain. This was the vision, but when I stepped outside the front door, the reality was different. Apart from the trees that Gregory and his father had planted, my quarter of an acre looked like a builder's yard, with piles of gravel and rubble everywhere, and quantities of broken tiles. Dimitri's neat fencing only accentuated the wasteland from which my house rose. On further inspection, I noticed that the water outlet from the sink was a blue plastic pipe, which led above ground to next-door's orange grove. It leaked, so, growing on the bare ground around it was the only bit of greenery, mostly comprising broom and nettles. Indeed, one morning, I saw a flock of yellowhammers pausing in their flight to feed off the seeds. Had they flown down, as I had done, hoping to escape the northern winter?

Yellowhammers apart, SOMETHING HAD TO BE DONE. I looked at the contract, where Veronica had spotted the clause about tree-planting, but I could find no mention of workmen being obliged to clear up the site after the house was erected. Oh well!! Rather than confront Gregory, I bought a spade and a fork at the hardware store in Nafplion and tried to tidy up the ground myself. The spade was a Greek one, with a long handle, which was kind to my chronically fragile back. I dug into a pyramid of gravel at least a metre high, so that the car could be parked nearer to the house, but after a morning's work, I'd only moved a fraction of it and I was worn out.

Not to be outdone, I decided to diversify and tackle the garden proper. In my mind, I had planned that a major item would be a mass of purple bougainvillaea, which I could train to cover the entire North wall eventually. I began to dig a hole, but the rocky ground resisted. My hands were already blistered from my efforts with the gravel, and trying to get a purchase with a fork on this new site was painful.

"*Kalimera, Kiria*"

I looked up. It was Dimitri, Dimitri of the fencing, who

was so proud to have helped the English defeat the Communists in Athens, and who had given me grapes with pips in.

"Is it you have trouble?" he asked in broken English.

I straightened up and leaned on the fork.

"*Malister.*" (yes)

"Much rock. *Poli skliro.*" (very hard)

With a mixture of English and Greek and a graphic mime, he explained that I would never be able to grow anything on my ground. It had less than two inches of soil, covering rocky fragments, which extended beyond the boundary. So that was why Gregory and father had planted the trees round the edge of my property, where there were a few pockets of deeper soil! Dimitri stood there in his faded dungarees, chewing tobacco and looking at me with sympathy, or was it contempt? Then he turned away.

"Adios, Miss."

I watched his retreating figure walking towards the village of Agios Adrianos. Would he regale that macho crew playing backgammon in the café with the story of how the stupid Englishwoman had been hoodwinked? Let them laugh if they want to, but I was determined not to be downhearted.

Come on, I told myself, there's more to life than gardens, and I turned my attention to the veranda. This was reached from ground level by two steps, which brought it up to a level with the inside rooms of the house, and it was paved with the same white tiles. This meant that I could wheel my new butler's trolley (as it is called in leafy English suburbs), onto the veranda for snacks and drinks, and, moreover, there was a balustrade on the outside edge, to prevent anyone falling on to the rough ground below. Thwarted in my expansive plans for a garden, this veranda would have to serve as my patio. I already had a splendid geranium in a pot outside the front door, and I added two white plastic troughs, and filled them with a mixture of earth and compost bought from the garden centre in Nafplion. I also bought two dozen more of the geraniums, choosing ones in full flower, so that I could enjoy them immediately. Then, a few evenings after Dimitri's bombshell, I sat outside in one of the Tuffin's chairs, with a gin and tonic in my hand, and looked out at the incredible view of the plain of Argos. Right on time, I heard the sound of the shepherd and his flute, and then I saw him come round the corner with his gold-fronded sheep. I sipped my gin and breathed a sigh of contentment. I had done well to leave behind those cold Welsh hills. Just like the yellowhammers, I was onto a good thing, and so were they.

But I congratulated myself too soon. Overcome one problem, and another inevitably appears. This new one had more to do with gender than the rocky terrain. I must explain that, in order to drive to Nafplion, I had to pass through Gregory's village of Agios Adrianos, and I hated doing this because of the local *taverna*. The men, (and the customers were all men) preferred to drink their coffee or ouzo inside the dark little cavern which passed for a café, whiling away the time by playing dominos or *tavli*, a type of backgammon. I was predisposed to be critical of them because I knew that, while they were idly wasting their time, their women would be working in the house, or out in the fields. Perhaps they felt this antipathy, because as I drove by, they would look up slowly, with smouldering eyes, and exude a wordless menace. Where was the famed Mediterranean warmth, the welcoming smile? I would have preferred the equally famed bottom-pinching to such hostility. I began to wonder if I was being over-sensitive, but, one day, I had reason to go into the café to ask for directions. The man behind the bar was polishing glasses. He didn't look directly at me and only replied grudgingly, and the

half a dozen men sitting at the tables stopped talking until I
went back to the car. As I switched on the ignition, I heard
mocking laughter from the café, and knew that I was the
target. The recent meeting with Dimitri meant that they would
now have even more to snigger about. I felt pretty sure that
they would not have dared treat a foreigner in such a way if he
had been a man.

What the hell! I hadn't come to Greece to do battle with its
macho side, nor yet to make a garden. I'd come for its
weather, its history, and its fabulous scenery. One bright
morning, studying the Greek equivalent of an Ordinance
Survey Map, I saw that there was an interesting islet about four
miles west of Profitis Ilias. The hills rose up directly from the
shore, forming a sea lake with only a narrow exit to the Gulf
beyond, so I set off to explore. I followed a path that skirted
the village and led me up a slope, until I was out of sight of
any buildings. I breathed in the morning air, walking through a
wood of spindly alders, the soft sunbeams nudging through the
dappled leaves. Everywhere, there were tiny blue birds with
tiny voices, and the ever present smell of thyme. As I walked
the meandering track, I thought how my feet were now being
added to the countless others, which had flattened it for
countless centuries. There was no sound in the green-scented
air, just the heady absence of sound, and my feet touched the
ground lightly. Then I heard a sibilant hiss.

"*Mia Yeenaika!*" (a woman)

A stone's throw away, a couple of Greeks were harvesting
olives. I would have noticed them earlier, if my head had not
been in the clouds. They had put a tarpaulin on the ground
under a tree and they were beating the branches with sticks, in
order to dislodge the purple olives. Their heads were covered,
to protect them from the fruit as it fell. It was a sight as old as
time, but it was interrupted, when they turned and stood there,

sticks in hand, and looked at me accusingly.

"*Yeenaika*," I heard again, and thought I picked out the word "*moni*" (alone).

I fled the scene, but as I carried on through the trees, I could feel their censure boring into my retreating back. In spite of the incident, I forced myself to continue with my plan, and the inlet was as breathtaking as I had hoped. The sea insinuated itself into the layers of hills, blue upon mauve, mauve upon purple, but I knew that I would never go there again, because from that time on I restricted my wanderings to short trips near home. To a rural Greek, a woman alone is an anathema, it upsets the divine order, and even a foreign woman is subject to this censure. I had felt it before, in the sideways glances and muted insinuations, and once I was back in the safety of my house, the first doubts began to creep in. Had I made a mistake in coming here? Should I have chosen to live in a less rural area? Would I ever come to terms with these dark descendants of an ancient people?

Chapter 14

Winter Woes and an Intruder

It was now early October, and when I went out onto the veranda, I noticed that there was an ominous nip in the air. This wasn't supposed to happen. In Wales, yes, I would expect to observe the first signs of winter, but in sunny Greece? Also, I noticed that my limbs were beginning to creak a little, a condition I thought I had left behind with the cold and the damp of those northern climes. I am usually an indefatigable optimist, but now, coupled with the disappointment of the garden and unsatisfactory brushes with the natives, this downturn of the weather made me begin to doubt the validity of my whole enterprise. These doubts evaporated as soon as the sun came out, and although there was the occasional downpour, and sometimes at night the wind rattled the shutters, every day turned out cloudless and warm, and my washing still dried outside within an hour.

October turned into November, and the weather had only slightly deteriorated. I supposed that this was winter proper, and congratulated myself that I was now experiencing a Greece the package tourists would never have the privilege of knowing. Greek winter, with its bracing early mornings, was still better than the average British summer. But, to my cost, I learnt that this situation would not last. Unknown to me, a north wind, called the *bora,* was massing in the Balkans and travelling south. It had already reached Salonika in the north of Greece, and was sending the average temperature there to below freezing. It was rapidly heading for the Peloponnese. I began to feel the relentless advance of the cold and, by mid-November, I was wearing most of the warm stuff I had brought with me, stuff that I had thrown in as an afterthought, when I was packing. Soon, I was colder than I had ever been, with a cold that penetrated several layers of wool, and I noticed that even the Greeks were muffled up in bonnets and gloves. I appealed to Gregory. He was, after all, my agent, in spite of our difference of opinion. His parent's house had a wood-burning open fire and several solar panels, and looking around, I saw that most post-war houses had been fitted with them. Why hadn't he fitted at least one of them to mine? He brushed aside the question and suggested portable gas heaters, so I bought a couple, with the accompanying cylinders, at the hardware store. They made a difference but they didn't heat the main room as well as I had hoped, so I turned to the central fireplace.

"My friend Christos will bring you some wood," said Gregory loftily.

Since our little 'misunderstanding', he had adopted a superior attitude, as if I had been the transgressor. Christos came with a truckload of logs and dumped them on the building site. He charged me the equivalent of £300, which I thought was a bit steep, but I was prepared to pay anything to be able to turn my ice-box into a comfortable living space. I bought a sack of kindling from a friendly carpenter in Nafplion, and carefully began to light a fire. Paper first, then the kindling, and when it was alight, I put on a couple of Christos' logs. I blew gently on the fire and then "drew" it with a sheet of newspaper, but the logs wouldn't ignite. I even tried a splash of paraffin to encourage them, but they remained sluggish. Instead of a blazing fire, I had a pitiful apology, which smoked out the living room. Over the next few weeks, I tried several times to light a fire, thinking that perhaps the logs were damp, or the chimney faulty, but I never succeeded in getting a satisfactory blaze going. Much later, I discovered that the logs were from Christos' apricot orchard, and apricot wood is notorious for being impossible to burn. So much for friend Christos!

Without an adequate fire, I was forced to make do with the gas cylinders, running them on maximum, which meant that they had to be renewed frequently. I had no problem loading the empties into the car and taking them to Nafplion, but it was a major performance getting the full ones out of the car and carrying them back indoors. I still couldn't drive right up to the house, because of the builder's rubble, so I had to 'walk' each cylinder along the ground and up the two steps to the veranda, frequently in the lashing rain. I wondered what my friends back home would think if they saw the reality of my life in Greece, soaked from the lashing rain after struggling with the cylinders, then, later, sitting at the computer, with the windows tightly closed and shuttered, flanked on either side by two gas heaters, and wearing an overcoat and a woolly hat. I should have cut my losses, given up and gone home, but as my ex-husband used to say during our frequent arguments,

"You're too damned stubborn. You never know when to give up."

Perhaps he was right, poor, misunderstood, misbegotten Deryk.

It was now mid November, and I reasoned, stubbornly or otherwise, that there were only three more months to go before my planned return to Wales, and before then I would be able to experience the famed Greek Spring that the poets eulogise about. Surely that was worth waiting for, and worth putting up with the present inconveniences! I decided to go into Nafplion on the following day and buy a third gas heater, but the following day dawned with another disaster. After a suspiciously quiet night, no wind, no banging of shutters, I looked out of the widow and saw – SNOW. Snow in southern Greece! Nobody had prepared me for this! Alright, snow in Albania, where the Greeks had repelled the Albanians in WWII, but not snow in the Peloponnese. For goodness' sake, Nafplion wasn't far from Crete and Crete wasn't far from Africa! I went outside and took some photographs, to convince people in Wales that this had really happened. Of course, it was very beautiful, the olive trees especially, their deep green leaves covered with the white stuff and their purple fruit transformed, but I was incensed by the unfairness of nature. I was even more incensed when I discovered that my unprotected drain pipe was frozen, and the sink and bathwater didn't drain away. Bloody Gregory, I don't like you, and I don't like your house, and I wish I'd never set eyes on Nafplion!

But there were compensations, and these outweighed the irritations. I had at last been accepted by the neighbouring farmer and his family, and, one night, I was invited to supper. It was very agreeable and patriarchal, with Tassos holding court at the head of the table, slicing with a long knife the flat batch, which he held against his chest, and offering me, as guest of honour, the choicest pieces of meat. His wife was welcoming, the children charming, and the home-made retsina was better than any I could buy in a shop. This was what I had come for, this camaraderie, this integration, enhanced by the fact that it had nothing to do with Gregory and his family. Indeed, Tassos made a mild comment about Pappa Yannis and his penchant for ouzo. I walked home, feeling that the long isolation was over, and looking forward to many such encounters.

The Tassos farm was next door to mine but obscured from my sight by a slight slope in the road. As I came to the top of the rise, I saw that the lights were on in my house and that the windows were open. Gregory? A surprise visitor? I stepped up on to the veranda and saw through the window that there was a strange man inside. He looked up and our eyes met, and with one bound, he jumped through the window, knocking me over as he did so. I screamed and he ran on without stopping, through the gate and along the SAME PATH that I had just used. I got up and saw his dark shape disappearing over the hill, like a black bat, or like the dreaded Stringloss★, the fiend of local legend. Now came the hardest part. No one had heard my scream and I would obviously have to go back to Tassos' house to get help, but that would mean retracing the same route that my intruder had just taken. Would he lie in wait and spring out on me before I could reach it? I stepped out cautiously, looking from side to side, and then went bravely through my gate and onto the road. It was empty and there flashed into my mind the lines from Coleridge's *Rime of the Ancient Mariner*, which had terrified me when I was a child:

> *Like one that on a lonesome road*
> *Doth walk in fear and dread,*
> *And having once turned round walks on*
> *And turns no more his head;*
> *Because he knows a frightful fiend*
> *Doth close behind him tread.*

Was Stringloss indeed behind me? I broke into a run and arrived at Tassos' house, breathless and panicked, and blurting out the situation in incoherent Greek. Tassos was calming and sympathetic, and walked back with me to the house. He went through every room and looked around the garden, then he told me to lock myself in securely.

★ Stringloss. One of many types of "exotica" (spirits, witches, demons) found in folklore. Stringloss is usually associated with death.

Chapter 15

Stalemate

I hardly slept that night and was thankful when dawn came. I opened the front door, hoping to breathe in comfort from the morning air, and wondering if I had dreamt the whole night's episode, when I saw a pack of playing cards strewn across the veranda. Had they been there the night before? Had the intruder dropped them in his flight, or, my God, had he come back again after I had gone to bed? I very gingerly picked them up until I had the whole pack in my hand, then, turning to look at the other side, I nearly dropped them all again. Each one was a representation of a sexual coupling, some with two people, and some with three. I couldn't tell whether they were paintings, or photographs of real people, but they certainly exhibited a fertile imagination, and I would never look upon the term "calling card" in the same way again. I tried to remember the brief impression I had of the man as he dashed past me through the window. Who was this intruder? Was he a nutter, a rapist, or a misogynist?

The cards were the final straw, and I felt shaken and vulnerable, but I went back into the house and forced myself to behave normally: bath, breakfast etc. then, at ten o'clock, I went to Gregory's office. He was out, having gone to

Kalamata, and Pappa Yannis was sitting in for him. We carried on a bizarre conversation in fractured Greek, and he may or may not have understood what I was trying to explain, but eventually, with the help of a dictionary and manic mimicry from me, he got the gist of the situation. Then, I showed him the pack of cards. He took them and solemnly studied them, lingering over each one. Was this a new experience for him, or had he heard of worse things in the Confessional? What would be the standard absolution for participants in any of these graphic encounters?

"*Perno avto, Kiria,*" (I'll take these") he said, putting them in his pocket.

I stood aghast! My evidence was going to disappear!

"What about the police?"

He shook his head vigorously, "No, no, oh no."

I needed Gregory and Gregory's facility with English to help me with this urgent problem. I champed around Nafplion, waiting for him to get back from Kalamata, and when he arrived, tousled and chewing toffees, I poured out the whole story and demanded that he take me to the police station and report the intrusion.

"No, no, oh, no," he said echoing his father.

What was this? A Greek conspiracy?

"A man broke into my house, a burglar," I argued.

"Did he take anything?"

"No, but…"

Gregory talked rapidly to his father then turned to me triumphantly.

"We think that there's no need to go to the police."

How could I explain to these uncomprehending men that I had felt violated and that I was terrified of it happening again? I got up from the chair and mustered all my resources.

"Then I will go myself," I said.

This roused them.

"Come and have some coffee, " said Gregory, gently guiding me out of the office.

We went to a nearby café and he explained, over the tiny steaming cups, that they knew who the intruder was. He was the village idiot, son of the local baker.

"He's harmless," said Gregory, "nothing to worry about. More coffee?"

They had closed ranks, but where did that leave me? They knew who this man was, but I didn't. From now on, I would be regarding every male in the area with suspicion, and I asked myself, when would he strike again? The whole incident illustrated the gender gap and the differing values between Greek and British society. A woman had no rights in Greek eyes, the local nut-case had priority over her sensitivity, and, sadly, it would always be like this. I decided that I must get out now, before this macho culture engulfed me. Although I was not yet prepared to consider selling, I was certainly prepared to ditch the Greek Spring and bring forward my plan to leave for Wales at the first possible moment.

I skulked at home for a few days, making plans for an early departure. I would present Gregory with a *fait accompli* once I had bought my plane ticket. THEN, I WENT ON A SHOPPING TRIP TO NAFPLION. Passing near the "black sails" restaurant, I noticed that there was some sort of ceremony going on in front of the harbour. There were hundreds of people gathered there, clad in their winter clothes, and bobbing in and out among them was the entire population of the flat-topped priesthood of Nafplion. Some were holding chalices, some were swinging incense, there was a good deal of intoning in Katharevousa, formal Greek, instead of the usual Demotic, and the air was pungent with smoke and holiness. I couldn't understand the words but I realised that the ceremony was working up to a climax. The crowd pressed forward to the very edge of the water, and a richly dressed priest with a mitre on his head kissed a gold ring and threw it into the sea. There was an orgiastic sigh from the crowd, and I found the hairs on the back of my neck begin to stand on end...

When he was on his way to the Trojan War, Agamemnon had sacrificed his daughter Iphigenia at a place called Aulis, in order to encourage the winds to fill the sails of his becalmed ships. Was Agamemnon already hooked on this way of propitiating the gods? Had he done it before, but in a less drastic form? What about the small fleet of ships that he had assembled, right here on this beach, as they were preparing to set off and join the others at the assembly point in Euboea? Did he indulge in his favourite pastime and make a sacrifice for good weather on this very spot, not a human sacrifice this time, but a precious object such as a ring? Again, I had this overwhelming feeling of the distant past leaning out and touching the present. What were my problems, set in the context of the last three thousand years?

I couldn't leave this place, not for good, anyway, but I would have to readjust my plans. This time, I'd stick it out until February, and go home to Wales for the Spring, but I was determined not to spend another winter in Greece. I would cut short my Welsh visit this time, and return to the villa in July, staying until the beginning of November, and when the cold weather came, I would fly home to my Welsh cottage, where at least there were adequate provisions against the elements. It wasn't an admission of failure, I told myself, more an adjustment to fit in with the circumstances. Satisfied with this arrangement, I settled contentedly for the few remaining months in Greece, and succeeded in partially blotting out my distaste for Greek men. There were no more nightly intruders. Perhaps, the village elders, or more likely Pappa Yannis, had warned off the baker's crazy son, so maybe it was best that we hadn't brought in the police. Incidentally, Pappa Yannis kept the playing cards.

Chapter 16

Writing Again

"Tell me now, you Muses that live on Olympus, since you are goddesses and witness all that happens, whereas we men know nothing that we are not told – tell me who were the captains and chieftains of the Danaans (Greeks)?"

Homer then makes out a list of the armies that lined up to fight the Trojans. It goes on for pages, and in the list are the Provinces of the Peloponnese: Corinth, Mycenae, Epidavros etc. – and included in these pages is the phrase: "the citizens of Argos and Tiryns of the Great Walls." The ruins of Tiryns lie only four miles from Nafplion, so, one day, I took the short bus ride to look at them. Tiryns has a military air, with a sweeping curved entrance, wide enough to take two chariots abreast. The ramparts are made of enormous stone blocks (Homer's walls), each as big as a small shed. Legend has it that they were constructed by the Cyclops, mythical one-eyed giants, who alone could have had the strength to lift them. Inside the fortress, the stone-flagged courtyard has small rooms branching off, linked by *syrinx* or galleries. These were arched, rather like the cloisters in Gloucester Cathedral, but they looked more precarious, not being fixed together by any sort of mortar. I was tempted to walk through one of these galleries, but was put off when I saw a couple of iron braces that had been recently put up to reinforce the Cyclopean handiwork. My caution proved to be justified because, a week later, when I returned with my camera, the entrance gate was shut. There was a notice displayed on it which read,

"Owing to an unfortunate fall of stone, these premises will be closed until further notice."

What was it Hamlet said? "Oh, my prophetic soul!" Had I been prophetic the previous week? That's what comes of living cheek by jowl with Elijah!

Balked of my photographic trip, and having missed the bus, I walked back to Nafplion; and as I walked, I imagined Agamemnon and his soldiers treading the same path on their way to the nearest embarkation point, the harbour where I had recently seen the Greek Orthodox ceremony. Having spent their last night on Greek soil at Tiryns, they would have set off with their horses and shields and siege equipment to embark onto the waiting triremes. Then, they would wait impatiently for a fresh wind to take them down the Argolic Gulf, past the Pharos (lighthouse) at Sounion, and on to the island of Euboea, where they would meet up with Menelaus and the rest of the Greek fleet. Agamemnon would have said goodbye to his wife and daughter, Clytemnestra and Iphigenia, who had come down to the harbour to see him off. Maybe, he promised to bring them some presents from Troy when he returned.

"Early next year," he might have said, as he kissed them goodbye.

I imagined the two women watching the ships get smaller as the fleet sailed away to the horizon, and I wondered how those men of Argos felt. Was it like it had been in my own time, when the ships sailed out of Southampton, as part of "Operation Overlord", to invade Normandy? Were the Greeks as excited and at the same time apprehensive as our own modern soldiers had been? The Greeks certainly didn't expect that the adventure would drag on for the next ten years, and that, in aeons to come, the whole enterprise would be mythologised. I remembered Tennyson's *Ulysses,* which describes the stragglers who returned:

> *We are not now that strength that in old days*
> *Moved earth and heaven; that which we are, we are*
> *One equal temper of heroic hearts*
> *Made weak by time and fate, but strong in will*
> *To strive, to seek, to find and not to yield.*

Having bought some milk and bread at Nafplion, I waited at the bus stop in the shadow of Palamidi for the twice daily bus back to Profitis Illias. I had been reduced to bus transport because my Mini was being serviced, and, in any case, I welcomed the experience of finding out alternative ways of getting around. But sitting doing nothing on the homeward bus, and passing through the dried and brittle winter landscape, I began to think about my neglected computer, and wonder whether I should do a bit more striving myself. I hadn't touched it for weeks, and the autobiography had reached an impasse. I was finding it difficult to describe the change from adolescence to maturity without using hindsight. When I got indoors, I made a cup of tea and paced the room. Something had to be done to get me started again, something to overcome the soul-destroying writer's block. As I reflected on the events of the afternoon, I realised that what was needed was a counter inspiration. As a change from autobiography, perhaps I should try and write some fiction. It didn't have to be too intense, more a sort of pot-boiler, which I could dash off in a couple of months. I realised, then, that the subject matter was staring me in the face. Why shouldn't I use the situation at Tiryns to write a modern thriller involving smuggling and murder? What about WHO PUSHED THE STONE as a title? No, maybe that would be a little too Biblical. How about DEATH IN GREECE? I sat down at the computer and began immediately. Two days later, I had typed 1500 words and was feeling very pleased with myself, and the story was coming along beautifully. The subject matter was all around me; how could I fail? My autobiography was put on hold while I concentrated on this new venture.

With something to occupy me, the days toward the tail end of winter passed delightfully, Christmas came and went, but not before I had been invited to Christmas lunch with the Tassos family: father, mother, two small daughters and an older daughter and son-in-law. The weather gradually became warmer, and I worked on the book each morning, and went shopping or visiting Magda in the afternoons., I re-visited Tiryns several times, to check up on a few details, the curator having given me access. My first idea was for the murder to be committed by someone heaving a heavy stone over the parapet and on to a rival below. On inspection of the site, I realised that this wouldn't work, because the parapet was too high. The murderer would have to be hiding in one of the *syrinx* (galleries) and attack the victim from behind. Of course, this was only a story, and the setting didn't have to be accurate, but I was inclined to be meticulous as to detail. This was another of my personal traits that my "ex" hated. After each visit to Tiryns, I went home and adjusted certain chapters, until I was sure that I had got them right.

In the more mundane world of Profitis Illias, my hopes of integrating with the locals had not really been fulfilled. Apart from the occasional wave from a passer-by, my only contact in the hamlet was with the Tassos family. After that Christmas dinner, I had often been to supper with them, including the "night of the intruder". Tassos was a lean, hard peasant, a farmer and the employer of the flute-playing shepherd. He also had orchards of oranges and olives. The oranges were small and full of pips. Whether that was due to their particular strain, or to bad husbandry, I never found out. He was very proud of his two young daughters, who went to school in Nafplion and spoke tolerable English. I imagined that they would leave home, when they were able, and taste the delights of Athens. In Greece there is no schism between town and country. Scratch any city slicker and you will find a peasant underneath. Most feast days are celebrated back in the villages, and relatives come from all over Greece, in order to return to their roots. Accountants and professors mix with subsistence farmers and shepherds, with no sense of strain on either side, the bonds of family being much stronger than any transient inequalities. For example, I had heard that Yannis, the shopkeeper brother of the musician Miki Theodorakis, could go home to the island of Chios and be accorded the same respect as his famous sibling.

My contact with Tassos and his wife was useful in helping me with problems that inevitably cropped up from time to time. For example, when Tassos discovered that I was going back to Wales for the next few months, he offered to garage my car.

"You can bring it here," he said, "and I'll put it in the barn. It will be safe there."

I thanked him and decided to bring him back something on my return, but what can you bring a happy and contented man, who lives in the sunshine, in a peaceful hamlet, surrounded by sweet smelling herbs and orange blossom?

Although I was often invited to the Tasso household, I would have hesitated to drop in on them unannounced. Not so with Gregory's mother, Magda. She was always welcoming and she would often leave whatever she was doing and take the opportunity to sit with me and drink coffee and gossip. By now, my Greek had improved considerably, and we would sit by the log fire, it still being winter, and Magda would proudly show me photographs of the family. She had a new grandchild, of whom she was very proud, and a son-in-law who was in the army. Strangely, there were no childhood photographs of Gregory. Had he sprung fully grown from the womb, like Pallas Athene? Perhaps that was his problem; he had missed a normal childhood and was having to make up for it now. Poor Gregory. I was sure was a very nice person inside, but it hadn't quite formed yet. I was very fond of Magda, and Magda, on her part, took great pleasure in giving me small gifts of flowers, home-made biscuits, oranges (without pips), and once, even, a small china ornament of two lovebirds that I have still in my bedroom in Wales.

One bright morning, we decided to have another go at the Wednesday market; this time, with no confusion over the clocks going back. I took the opportunity to buy presents to take back to Wales, light in weight, because I would be flying. I wandered among the stalls and bought pots of mixed herbs, a mug with the word "Nafplion" on it, several bamboo flutes for my grandchildren, and, finally, a large bottle of ouzo for Gareth, the Welsh neighbour who was looking after my house.

Towards the end of January, the Greek Spring began to unfold, very slowly, with crocuses pushing up through the rocks, the buds on the fruit trees opening, and overall an intoxication of scents. I decided that my last expedition before I left would be to visit Veronica's Epidavros staging post. I climbed over the boulders, arrived at the top, and looked at the impressive view. I could see Nafplion and its harbour, the fortress of Tiryns, the Argolic Gulf, and a glimpse round the corner of the distant hills of Argos. As I breathed in the ever present scent of thyme, I felt privileged to be standing there. Greece, with her layers of history, had allowed a woman from a Philistine island between two cold seas to own a small part of herself. Did it matter that my bit was rocky and infertile, and that the surrounding populace was priest-ridden? Surely, the charm of their religion was its very craziness: the ambivalence of the priests, the flaking murals on the Byzantine walls, the black clad women kissing unhygienic icons. I was glad that I had decided to keep the house and come back again next July. As I stood there on that ancient elevation and surveyed the scene, I knew I couldn't turn my back on all the glory that surrounded me, of which I had become part.

The time came when I was to leave for Wales. I said goodbye to a tearful Magda, and promised to bring her on my return a hand-made rug that my middle daughter, Penelope, had woven.

"Penelope," said Magda. "A Greek name; we sometimes shorten it to Poppy."

The final goodbye to Gregory could not be avoided; he was, after all, my agent, my representative in Nafplion. Lately, his attitude to me had mellowed into a wary friendship and, who knows, maybe he was relieved to be let off the role of a typical Greek stud. I knew that his other obsession still remained: the house. He still felt drawn towards it, but I argued that this possessiveness would be assuaged while I was away, because he could look at its emptiness and feel that it belonged to him. I gave him the spare keys, and he saw me off on the bus to Athens. I boarded the British Airways flight at the international terminal with a light heart, confident that, in spite of everything, my revised plan was going to work.

Chapter 17

Squatters

As I travelled on the train from Paddington to Shrewsbury, and then continued on the little Welsh line to my cottage, I watched the scene unfold through the carriage windows, and I congratulated myself on the fact that I had just achieved a small miracle. I was experiencing a double Spring. With the Greek one behind me, I knew that here the flowers would be pushing up through the resisting earth; snowdrops, aconites, wild crocuses, I noticed that there were buds on the trees, passing hedgerows were sprinkled with hawthorn blossom, like forgotten snow, and soon the daffodils would begin their annual nodding display. Opening my door the following morning, I was conscious of the welcome sound of birds of all sizes, many more than in Greece: tiny sparrows, dunnocks, robins, chaffinches, and, high above, crows and buzzards and an occasional red kite. The sounds they made were inversely proportional to their size, the buzzards only emitting a thin "Whee", whereas the song of a tiny robin perched on the post of my clothes line reverberated across the valley. I saw no yellowhammers, and wondered at what speed small birds fly. Perhaps I had passed them on the way, perhaps at this moment they were resting on a green patch in Northern France. When they eventually arrived, would they brag to the stay-at-home robins about the distance they had travelled?

The subsequent weeks in the Principality were occupied with catching up; airing the house, visiting friends, rescuing the overgrown garden. I even went to the theatre! It was a play at Theatr Hafren in Drenewydd (Newtown), about Robert Owen, a local nineteenth century benefactor. I also had to admit grudgingly to myself that I felt a sense of liberation, a lifting of tension and restrictions, as I went about doing everyday familiar things. I could roam the hills on my own and not feel nervous; I could go into a pub on my own and feel welcomed; I could meet male friends on a basis of equality, and I could buy any amount of Cadbury's chocolate, and umpteen types of tea. Above all, I enjoyed the casualness of officialdom, the friendly policemen, and the helpful telephone operators. It was ironic that Greece, the so-called birthplace of Democracy, was now hide-bound by religion and male domination and tortuous bureaucracy. Why did Greece still have such a hold over me? Why hadn't the last year dented my original enthusiasm? Why was I fretting to get back there? Which of the gods was beckoning me: Apollo, Aphrodite, or flute-playing Pan?

Despite this bewildering mixture of loyalties, I enjoyed my few months at home and catching up with family news and gossip, but I was more than ready to depart by the end of June. I sent a fax to Gregory via the our local post office, gave my neighbour Gareth the key of my cottage, and flew to Athens. From there, I took the local bus to Leoforia Peloponnesa, and boarded the coach for Nafplion. A Staithos taxi was waiting to take me along the dusty road to Profitis Illias, and I was soon standing in my pine-panelled living room. I made a hot drink, nibbled a Ryevita, went to bed, and slept dreamlessly.

I woke to a perfect morning; a pale sun cast long shadows

across my private wilderness. I opened the wooden shutters and went out on to the veranda. The geraniums had obviously been blooming bravely, but the blossoms now looked a little tired, so I deadheaded them, to encourage more flowers to grow. Then, looking across to the end of the garden, I saw that the lemon tree was wilting and clearly hadn't taken root, maybe Pappa Yannis should have shovelled in more soil. Never mind, the sun was shining, and I wheeled out the trolley for breakfast on the veranda. I rummaged in my store cupboard for tea-bags and long-life milk and, although I found them, the rest of the cupboard looked strangely bare. Maybe I hadn't stocked it as thoroughly as I remembered, but then, on straightening up, I looked around the room and noticed that the furniture had been moved. Surely, the sofa used to be under the right-hand window! At that moment, a shutter slipped off its hook and hung askew. I remembered that same shutter becoming unhinged during the strong winds last winter. When I went to hook it on to the wall again, I had the oddest sensation that someone had done this before.

I began to feel uneasy. Had I been invaded again, had there been another presence inhabiting my house, or was my imagination coloured by that very real intruder, the baker's son? I reasoned that the only one with a key was Gregory, and he had a perfectly good home to go to... unless, unless! It suddenly occurred to me that he may have found a girlfriend and turned my house into a little love nest, in which case, good luck to him, and no hard feelings, but who was this girlfriend? She could have been inquisitive, may even have been light-fingered, so I went through all my clothes cupboards and drawers, but nothing had been disturbed, even my rather déclassé vests were intact. Another thought struck me, I felt that something was missing, but I couldn't quite pin it down, then it came to me: WHERE WAS THE

SAMSONITE SUITCASE? It was the most expensive piece of luggage that I owned, and I had left it in Greece, rather that risk it on the flight to Wales. I searched frantically, under the beds, behind the pile of logs, in the bathroom, but there was no sign of it. As I straightened up, I could kid myself no longer; the evidence was irrefutable; someone had used this place in my absence, raided the larder, moved the furniture, and finally stolen a valuable suitcase. My previous tolerance towards Gregory's probable misuse evaporated, and I prepared to do battle.

I extricated my car from Tassos' barn, dispensing with the usual pleasantries. I'd do the thank you and present-giving when I got back. I drove to Nafplion, parked the car, and walked purposefully down the alley to Gregory's office. Of course, he wasn't there, I'd forgotten that he would never win any prize as an early bird. I should have called at the house, but that would have meant upsetting Magda, as I was determined to have it out with him when we met, even if it resulted in a slanging match. I filled the waiting time with toast and coffee, simultaneously trying to keep my fury on the boil.

"Hello," said Gregory, when we met at last. "Welcome. *Kalimera?*" (Good morning.)

"Someone's been using my house," I said aggressively. "Who was it? Why didn't you let me know?"

"*Siga, siga,*" (softly, softly) said Gregory nervously, as the man in the dry-cleaners looked up. "There's no problem," he continued. "I put in two of my workmen, two Poles."

"What! What right had you to let them take over my home?"

"Easy, easy," said Gregory. "They were there for security."

"Security!"

I was spitting with anger by now, and the dry-cleaner put down his iron to listen. Gregory answered me slowly as if he were speaking to a child.

"You must realise that it is dangerous here in early summer, when the Albanians come down for fruit picking. They are very untrustworthy; no unattended house is safe from them. I put in two of my workmen as protection."

"Untrustworthy are they!" I snorted. "What about your Poles? They've stolen a very expensive *mala* (bag) of mine."

Gregory looked hurt. "Oh no, no, not the Poles. You must have made a mistake."

"No mistake," I said firmly. "But let's ask them. Where are they now?"

"They, er, have gone to work on another site."

"Very convenient," I said sarcastically.

"Are you sure you left it in Greece? Are you sure you didn't take it to England?"

I stamped my foot. "Of course I'm sure! Do you take me for an idiot?"

Then I stopped. That is precisely what I had been taken for all these months, a clumsy, naive barbarian from a bleak island.

"Have some coffee," said Gregory, seeing me hesitate.

"I don't want any. Those Poles must have taken my suitcase."

"We'll go back to the villa and make a thorough check. I'm sure it couldn't have been them." said Gregory soothingly.

Huh, I thought, Poles OK, Albanians not, and the British? Ripe for picking, obviously! Gregory looked at his watch.

"I've just time to take you back to the house and have a good look for that *mala*."

What was there to lose? I went back, following his Volvo in my Mini, and the bag wasn't there. But I noticed something that I had missed before. Some of the tins of food had gone but others had been replaced, so the Poles had tried to play fair, after all, they just couldn't resist that splendid Samsonite bag. I turned to Gregory. He was standing in the middle of the room, wearing a smile that encompassed the high ceiling, the wood panelling, and the sun streaming in from the veranda. He reminded me of an artist revisiting a favourite painting.

"You like?" he said. "You like?"

"Oh for heaven's sake," I snapped. "You know I like, but there's no need to go on about it. And now, if you don't mind, I've got some unpacking to do. I'll call at your office tomorrow."

I went outside to unpack the Mini. He stood there, unbelieving; he'd never been spoken to like this before, and by a woman! I remained unrepentant as he manoeuvred the Volvo round the piles of rubble in the garden and disappeared over the hill. Next day, when I called on him, he huffily gave me some bills, including the water bill. When I went to the council offices and paid over the drachmas, I wondered casually how many Polish baths I was subsidising. A week later, two friends turned up in a bright green Landrover Discovery; they were on their way to Egypt.

Chapter 18

Bobbie and Marion

Bobbie and Marion are two feisty ladies, who live in adjacent villages in Wales, adjacent, that is, with a mountain in between. Roberta Korner, better known as Bobbie, lives in Cwm-y-Glaise (Blue Valley), and is the widow of Alexis Korner, the rock star. Marion Edwards lives in Cnwclas (Anglicised version Knucklas, there being no "k" in the Welsh alphabet), and, from time to time, she is a grass widow, when her husband, Peter, is out working on the oil rigs. A couple of weeks ago, when Peter was due to be away for some time, the two took advantage of his absence to drive from Wales to Egypt.

"Why Egypt?" I asked, when the metallic green Discovery crunched over the rubble to my back door.

"Well," said Marion, "we went to Egypt on that organised coach trip with Roger Bright's lot last year, and thought we'd try it again, on our own. Last time, they rushed us round a bit too quickly and we wanted to have a more leisurely go at the place. Luxor is something else and needs much more than a quick guided tour, and then there's Giza, which we didn't see at all."

"To say nothing of the dishy tour guide," said Bobbie

mischievously. "What was his name, Hassan?"

They laughed at the memory, like two schoolgirls.

"How was the trip here?" I asked, helping with the bags and feeling excluded.

"Fine," said Marion, who seemed to be head of the expedition. "We stayed at campsites, slept in the car once, and, finally, booked a hotel in Ancona, before taking the ferry to Patras."

"No problems?" I asked, still unable to believe that they had dropped in as if they only lived a few miles away.

"Only at Chamonix. The road was blocked with snow and we had to make a detour through Grenoble."

Grenoble was one of the places the train had passed through on my own car journey to Greece. I remembered all the stations: Boulogne-Paris-Lyon-Grenoble-Milan-Bologna, and decided there and then that my preferred way of travelling across Europe would always be with the assistance of French Railways. Bobbie and Marion were able to share the driving, and that would have made a difference.

"How will you get to Egypt?" I asked, prepared for any answer, however bizarre.

"Sail by ferry from Piraeus," said Marion. "We've booked it for a week from now."

Splendid, I thought. There'll be time to show them the sights, a good opportunity for the BIG ONE, the Palace of Mycenae, which I had been saving for just such an occasion. What had Schliemann said, as he opened the tomb at the grave circle?

"I have looked upon the face of Agamemnon."

That gold mask was now one of the most treasured exhibits in the museum in Athens, but the grave circle was still there at Mycenae, and much more beside.

However, even feisty women like Bobbie and Marion

needed a rest after their 1,500-mile journey, and, after a shower and a change of clothes, they relaxed on my veranda, seated in Tuffin's deck chairs, drinking gin and tonics, and watching the old shepherd pass by, leading his sheep, while the sky turned golden.

"The house is bigger than I thought," said Bobbie, "and much more spectacular. That view!"

The setting sun behind us threw long shadows across my sad patch of land, merging with the mist rising up from the plain of Argos, until the house itself and the three tipplers on the veranda seemed to be floating on an island, the echoes of the shepherd's flute giving a surreal otherworldliness to the scene.

Next morning, refreshed, we climbed into the Discovery and drove to Mycenae. How does one describe the indescribable? How dare one try to put into words a site that existed hundreds of years before Homer! Stones that have been warmed by suns that shone on the Neolithic hairy mammoth, stones that have seen the comets in their periodic orbits hundreds of times over! We walked through the Lion Gate, and on our right were the royal graves, slabs of upright stones set out like a WW2 cemetery, but instead of rows, they formed one big circle. When a king died, how did they extend the circle? Were the stones shuffled nearer together, to make space for the new arrival? Homer is silent on the subject.

We climbed the imposing, wide staircase to the top of the palace and the living quarters of the royal family. We even saw the bath where, according to the poet Aeschylus, the vengeful Clytemnestra drowned her husband Agamemnon, when he returned from the Trojan war. Outside the Lion Gate and beyond the ramparts, we tip-toed into one of the beehive tombs. These are great domes, curving to an apex more than fifty feet high, made of chunks of rock. Only gravity and their own cunning shapes hold the edifice together. We walked as if in a cathedral, and felt obliged to speak in whispers; even the irrepressible Marion was subdued. What did it matter that many of the stories had been fabricated, that Homer, Aeschylus and others had used much more than poetic licence, that Agamemnon, Achilles, Patroclus etc. were only men, maybe puny men at that? There was a certain something at Mycenae, the rocks exuded it. There was grandeur and a depth, which told of immense power, which time and decay had failed to destroy. After an exhausting afternoon, we climbed back into the car and drove home.

"Magic," said Bobbie. "Utter magic."

Meanwhile, in Nafplion and Profitis Illias, the word had gone round about the British visitors and their enormous car, and Gregory was soon inviting myself and my friends to lunch.

"You like?" he said, when he called, indicating my property as if it was his own. "You like?"

"Yes I like very much," said Bobbie tactfully.

Gregory didn't take us to the backstreet, businessmen's restaurant that had been the overture to my semi-seduction, but chose the big restaurant in Syntagma Square, with its outside tables and striped awning. This was a different Gregory from the nervous lover of that strange night up on Palamidi. Here was a dashing young Greek, relaxed, teasing, and flirtatious. Was it that he felt safer with three women, rather than one? Was it that he enjoyed cutting a dash by squiring three foreign ladies around the town, to say nothing of the shiny green Discovery? As we drove into the car park by the harbour, it had stood out among the Volvos and dusty Renaults. Quietly, cynically, Bobbie treated Gregory's heavy gallantry with politeness, but Marion, the brash, workaholic Brummie, egged him on to excessive pleasantries, only remarking to us when he was out of hearing,

"If he thinks he's going to get into our knickers after buying us a carafe of turpentine (retzina) and a few squid, he's got another think coming."

I said nothing. My friendship with the other two didn't extend to the deeper intimacies, and in telling them about the ups and downs of the past year, I had left out those few months when Gregory and I had been lovers. I did, however, enjoy sharing my other experiences, sounding them out against a couple of friends with the same background as mine, and comparing their reactions with my own.

"He actually broke into the house and they did nothing!"

"I bet Pappa what's-his-name looks through that pack of cards when he's having a quick tea break behind the altar!"

"The cheek! Fancy dumping his workmen in your house!"

We were now back on the veranda, having a sun downer before the final meal of their stay. Marion, the workaholic, the Brummie businesswoman, leaned back in her chair, after the second gin and tonic, and said casually,

"Why don't you do holiday lets?"

I was stopped in my tracks. "It never really occurred to me. I'll be using it during the summer and early autumn, possibly for a short visit, as well, in the Spring. The only time it will be empty is in the winter, when the weather is cold."

"I'm sure you were unlucky in that first winter," said Marion. " The Greeks say that they only get snow once or twice every ten years. What about trying to get some Germans? They're mad about Greece and they're usually very hardy?"

I'd already picked up the German obsession with Greece, mostly with nationals who had been the former occupiers in WW2. I gather they had been entranced by its beauty and culture, and although this didn't prevent them from perpetrating horrific atrocities, they now assumed, with typical German phlegm, that time is a great healer and that the Greeks would forgive and forget.

"We-el," I said, "they're better placed than the British. They're nearer and they can drive down overland, but do I want strangers in my house?

"You've already had them, duckie," said Marion. "And who's to stop lover boy from doing it again?"

Now Bobbie intervened; she had a spare house in Weymouth.

"I've tried letting in the past," she said, "but there are all sorts of problems. Arranging a cleaner, insurance, getting the dates right, and equipping the place with pots and pans. And people can be awkward. I had one couple who wanted the rate reduced because I hadn't provided egg-cups! And there's the privacy bit. Where do you put your personal things? Do you move them out, lock them away, or what? I gave up in the end."

But Marion was now hooked on her idea of letting, and used her considerable entrepreneurial experience, experience with which she had set up various ventures in Wales – a café, upholstery, hairdressing, hat-making – to try to convince me that all my problems would be solved if I went into the holiday lets business.

"But the bus only comes once a day, and there's only a sea view if you stand on tip toe at the top of the garden, and, anyway, there isn't a garden, and never likely to be.

"No problem transport-wise if they are German; they will have come down in their own car." She scooped up a handful of olives from the dish. "But I see your point about the garden," she continued. "It's shitty. You need something to deflect attention from it."

After a moment's reflection, she snapped her fingers. "Got it! What you want is a swimming pool."

"Oh no," I said quickly. "I've had so much expense already, I don't want to embark on anything else."

"Suit yourself," said Marion, "but that's my advice." She leaned over the veranda and spat out the olive pips.

The next morning, they were off. I watched them twisting upward round the bends until the vivid green roof of the Discovery dropped down the hill and out of sight. It had been a memorable and enjoyable visit, but it left me feeling uneasy. Marion was a very good business woman. Should I have listened to her advice?

Chapter 19

Swimming Pool (1)

Try as I might, I couldn't dismiss the ideas that they had left behind. The whirlwind visit had left me confused. I forced myself to look in a more realistic light at the rough, rocky piece of Greece that I had bought. The wilting trees, the poor, sparse soil, even the potted geraniums, couldn't disguise the fact that the immediate surroundings of the house were not attractive. I remembered Marion's words, "Why don't you do holiday lets? Why not have a swimming pool?"

Would a swimming pool help? Would this lure the gullible Germans? I realised that I must do something, otherwise I would be coming back year after year, feeling less than satisfied, and one day, maybe, even beginning to dislike the place. I turned the problem over in my mind for a couple of weeks. I was in a quandary, and the only ones who could have helped me make a decision were now crawling, behind Hassan, through the low tunnel to Khufuh's tomb in Giza. One morning, when the sky was eggshell blue, I made the decision.

"I want a swimming pool," I told Gregory.

He looked startled, as if I had suggested painting the house with red and blue stripes.

"I – I didn't think a pool would interest you," he said.

"Why, are there any snags?"

"Of course not," he replied, rather too quickly.

"My friends said it would put up the value of the house."

Gregory was aghast. "Do you intend to sell? I – I thought you liked the house, I thought you liked us."

"Of course I do, and I've no intention of selling, but I might let it sometimes, holiday lets, you know, and it would be easier to get tenants if there is a pool."

Satisfied that I had no plans for selling, and in spite of his initial hesitation, Gregory's business sense took over and he warmed to the idea.

"I built a pool for a Swedish client, not far from here. Would you like to see it?"

We drove to a small village by the sea and he showed me the Swede's swimming pool. It took up most of the garden of a little terraced house in a lane, and I realised that the setting was the opposite of mine. It was hemmed in on all sides by tiny, lime-washed houses, clothes lines, children, black clad women gossiping in doorways, and the inevitable bevy of cats. Would I have done better to have plunged myself into such a neighbourhood, instead of choosing my present rocky isolation? True, I had avoided the ex-patriot Brits, but had I thrown the baby out with the bathwater? Would life have been easier in this very Greek environment that the absent Swede seemed to have discovered? I shrugged off such thoughts. It was too late now, anyway, and so I inspected his pool. It was the right size, and I particularly liked the curved shape.

"What do you think?" asked Gregory.

"Yes, I like," I said. (Did he get the joke?)

"It's easy to maintain," he said. (No, he didn't.)

When we got back to the office, I asked him to draw up plans for a similar pool on my patch, then I went back to the house, to get ready for my end-of-season return to Wales. It was now late October, a month since Bobbie and Marion had left, and I wanted, at all cost, to avoid another bitterly unheated Greek winter. I again parked my car with Tassos and, by mid-November, I was sitting beside a roaring log fire, in my cosy Welsh cottage.

The tenor of life was slower back in Wales, with fewer decisions to make. My tiny garden needed very little attention, and I had long ago finished altering the inside of the house. There was time for reflection, and my thoughts turned to Gregory. Although I still resented his unspoken implication that our affair had been instigated by me, our new relationship was beginning to be more comfortable. To be fair, I had to admit that, in those early days, as far as a young Greek man was concerned, I had probably been giving out encouraging signs, by choosing to live alone, being anxious to be friendly, inviting him inside for coffee. These were all things that an inhibited Greek woman would never do. What was an unsophisticated local lad to think? I smiled to myself as I remembered my fury when he installed the Poles in my house, and I realised that I would have been much more forgiving if he had indeed used it as a love-nest. It would have exonerated me, having, as it were, opened the doors for him.

I fretted through the Welsh winter, watching the rain scudding across the purple hills, my mind constantly on the Greek house and Gregory. How was he getting on with the pool? He communicated with me far less now than when he was building the house, but a pool is a smaller undertaking. Around Christmas, I couldn't resist adding a note to the card I sent him.

"How is the pool getting on?"

He replied with a fax. "Still excavating. Rocks difficult to dislodge. *Chronia Pola.* (Happy New Year.)"

With this I had to be content. I could trust Gregory, on the building front at least. He had never let me down in that respect. Anticipating a completion within the next few months, I began to consider how I would manage the pool, once it became a reality. I remembered the words of Mr. Manolis in Paddington, as he was ogling my cleavage.

"It would be wise to get a local man to maintain the swimming pool."

From bitter experience, I wanted to cut down my reliance on Gregory, or any of his buddies. I still seethed at the thought of Chris and his apricot logs, and I certainly didn't want another thieving Pole. Then I thought, why should it always have to be a man, why not introduce woman power into the equation? Why shouldn't I do the job myself? Obviously, I'd have to learn the technicalities, and the sooner I found out about them, the better.

Trallwng (Welshpool) is a small country town in Mid-Wales, and based in one of its nearby villages is a firm called Colley Construction, which deals in the building and maintenance of swimming pools. Why such a firm should exist in poverty-stricken Wales was beyond my comprehension, but they were there, sure enough, in the classified part of the phone book. Perhaps their clientele came from rich Brummies from the Midlands, who had bought up second homes in our hills and wanted to embellish them. The English were getting more confident these days, since the militant "Sons of Glyndwr" had stopped burning holiday cottages. I reflected that, at least, there were no such activists in Greece. The locals, though reticent, were prepared to welcome foreigners, mainly because of the money they brought with them. But hang on, hadn't my negative experiences in Greece been a sort of house-burning? The harassment, the baker's son, the rip-offs? I put these disturbing thoughts aside and decided to call on Colley Construction for advice on pool management.

After driving a borrowed car through the twisting roads,

crossing and re-crossing the boundaries of the two border counties, in and out of Herefordshire and Shropshire and Powys, I came to a small village. In front of a house set back from the road, I saw a partially finished swimming pool, and knew that I had found the right place. I explained the situation to the company manager, and he was prepared to be helpful, even though I was not a prospective customer.

"This pool," he said. "What type of construction?"

"Er, I don't know."

He looked at me with a mixture of amusement and disbelief. I'd seen that look before, on Mr. Manolis, on Dimitri, on Gregory, and now on this man. He made a steeple with his fingers (where had I seen that before?), and spoke slowly and simply, as if to a child.

"There are two types of swimming pool: concrete blocks with a plastic lining, and one made with reinforced concrete, lined with tiles."

I thought quickly, I had to establish my credentials if he was to take me seriously. Then I remembered the pool in the Swede's garden; it had been lined with blue tiles.

"I remember now," I said. "It's a reinforced concrete one."

Mr. Colley, who I assumed it was, handed me a leaflet.

"You'll find most of what you want to know in this. Tricky business, pool maintenance. Your man will use chlorine as a sanitiser, of course, but in Greece, due to the temperature, he'll need to use a stabiliser as well. I would recommend Cyan uric acid. Will you be resident throughout the year? No? Then make sure he gives it a good dose of Algaecide occasionally, to inhibit green or black growth."

More affable now, he shook my hand and saw me to the car. His parting words were,

"You're lucky to have a place in Greece. When the pool is finished, send me a postcard and I'll come and look at it."

Chapter 20

Swimming Pool (2)

The visit to Colley's had been fruitful. I now understood more about the pool, how it was operated, and what I would have to do to keep it working. The information was rather daunting, and I wasn't sure if I would be able to maintain it on my own, but I was going to have a damned good try. Also, the spin-off was that I was better able to deal with the odd fax from Gregory and reply to it sensibly.

Fax from Gregory:	I'm placing the main drain towards the road. OK?
Reply from me:	So long as it doesn't go through the orange grove next door.
Fax from Gregory:	How high do you want the coping?
Reply from me:	6" above the last row of tiling.

Then, I couldn't resist a question of my own.

Fax from me:	What pH (acidity and alkalinity) scale are you aiming for?

If a fax could register astonishment, the terse following reply from Gregory would have done so.

Reply from Gregory:	pH7.2 to 7.8

After this, there was an ominous gap of two months. Had he taken umbrage? Then there came another communication.

Fax from Gregory: **Almost finished. When are you coming over?**

He must be short of cash, I thought cynically. The Welsh countryside that Spring was particularly beautiful, limpid green grasses, shallow streams winking over pebbles, buzzards wheeling in pairs high in the sky, even an occasional red kite, and the hedges were decked with hawthorn blossom, not like forgotten snow, as I had seen them from the train, but now in full bridal gear. I didn't want to leave it all, especially as the foxgloves promised to be particularly abundant that year, and I would miss the swathes of purple that would soon cover the hills. But curiosity prevailed, and at the end of May, I flew to Athens, earlier than planned. I climbed out of the Staithos taxi and carried my bag round to the front of the house, anxious to see the new addition to my property.

Just as my half built house had been a disappointment two years before, so was the sight of my new swimming pool, only, this time, the pool was not half built but almost finished. Why did I find it such a disappointment? For one thing, it was not curved as the Swede's had been, but was rectangular. However, I could live with that, and, moreover, Mr. Colley would have approved of the neat wooden housing for the pump and filter, and the blue tiled lining, but I remained depressed. Had I expected it to look like the glossy pictures in Mr. Manolis' brochures in far off Paddington? Come on, Eva, I told myself, this is a real live pool, which just happens to be empty, and a swimming pool without water is like a stage without scenery – the magic is missing. All it needed was to be filled up, and to have a scantily clad Veronica lolling back in a Tuffin's chair with a gin and tonic in her hand, to complete the picture. Except that the pool wasn't exactly empty. There

137

was a man with bare feet and rolled up trousers standing in it, in a puddle of rainwater and swollen cigarette butts. Instinctively, I knew who he was – one of the Poles! He looked up as I approached, grunted, spat on the blue tiles, and carried on rendering the coping stones. There was a proprietary air about him, as if he owned the place, and, indeed, he'd probably lived in my house as long as I had myself! Where had Gregory dumped the pair this time? What blissfully ignorant ex-pat was providing them with food and lodging? I wanted to shout across,

"*Pou einai a minha mala?*" (Where is my bag?)

Instead, I just nodded to the back of his sweat-stained shirt and unlocked the front door.

During the next few days, having paid Gregory something on account, and watched the pool finally finished, the coping completed, the tiles cleaned and polished, the steps fixed and the pumping system connected, I settled back into the Greek half of my life. I visited Magda, pottered around the shops in Nafplion, and sunned myself on the veranda. I also retrieved my car from Tassos, and gave him a small rug made by my daughter Penny, who was an expert weaver; it was similar to the one I had given Magda last year. He was polite but strangely taciturn, and I wondered why, but his wife Katerina was delighted.

"It's like the ones we used to make in the old days," she said.

As the weeks went by, and in spite of Tassos' reserve, I felt comfortable in my Greek home and believed that I was at last coming to terms with the neighbours. Accordingly, I decided to celebrate my return by inviting them to a soirée. I typed proper invitations and sent them out, to Dimitri, to Tassos and Katerina, to their elder daughter and her husband, who was a local teacher, and the two younger daughters. I went into

Nafplion and bought cakes from the patisserie, sweet pastries covered with icing sugar, and several bottles of light wine from the supermarket. When the appointed day came, I set out the goodies, put a Chopin medley into the cassette player, and waited. Would they come, or had I misinterpreted their friend-liness? During the afternoon, the bell from the church of Elijah rang and rang, one of the innumerable saint's days, I supposed. There were so many that I wondered that the Greeks hadn't begun to run out of names, but Christianity had been going for a long time. There were, too, the deities that Christianity had appropriated from the old Pagan rituals: St. Dennis for Dionysus, for example. Most of the saints had died horrible deaths – been roasted over slow fires, starved, chopped into pieces – I'd seen the frescoes on the walls at the monastery of Mistras. How did Christ put them back together again, I thought irreverently. Perhaps I should ask Pappa Yannis.

The gate clanged and they walked up the path in their best clothes: Dimitri in a clean white shirt, Katerina, elder daughter Maria with husband, the two small girls, but no Tassos. They sat awkwardly on the straight-backed dining chairs and declined both cakes and wine.

"We are fasting," said Maria's husband. "Today is the feast of St. Botom."

At least it sounded like Botom. So, if it was a feast, why didn't they eat my food? Conversation was difficult, as even the teacher spoke very little English. At last, under pressure, the two men drank a thimbleful of wine, and then the company backed out in an orderly manner and was gone, the gate clang-ing behind them. I kicked the loaded trolley with frustration, some soirée! Bloody Greeks, bloody blinkered Greeks! It was worse than Ireland! Perhaps I was a racist at heart. What had happened to Tassos? No one had explained his absence, I realised, as I wrenched the Chopin out of the cassette player.

Next morning, I drove to the gypsy encampment by the sea, and gave them all the cakes. At least they accepted them with grace, even though they tried to con me out of the pretty cake tin. On the way back, and still simmering but trying to think rationally, I decided once and for all that the gap between me and the Greeks was too great. I'd never be comfortable in this priest-ridden country. As I approached Nafplion, the roofs of the Orthodox churches were pricked out against the blue sky: Panagias, Agios Nicolaos, Agios Spiridon, Agios Georgios, Agios Konstantinos, Agios Trios. As I looked at them, I suddenly visualised the cherubic face of Pappa Yannis. He must have officiated at the service the day before, may even have rung that incessant bell, and greeted the faithful arriving in their Sunday Best, which I now realised wasn't for me but for him. How he must have laughed at my petty rivalry! Thinking back, I remembered the horrors of Lent, that first Spring. No meat, no fish, no bread, just complicated concoctions made from olives. Prayers day and night, and the infernal church bells, albeit muffled because of the approach of Easter. I'd watched people hurrying up the hill to early morning church, and even in semi-enlightened Nafplion there was a constant scurrying in and out of holy places, and black clad women kissing unhygienic icons. At the time, I thought it endearing, but now I realised how dark and sinister it was. There was no room for me in this alien country. I had to get out!

Where had the whole thing gone wrong? Probably, it began with that first cold snap from the Balkans. I should have abandoned the project right away, but I had stubbornly persisted, excusing each problem as it arose, and building up a faulty structure, which had now collapsed. How dared I have assumed that I could foist myself on a different culture, in a different land! Brief though the fateful soirée had been, it was the culmination of a series of disasters, which I had refused to accept at the time. I was now prepared to face reality, and things would never be the same again. THE DREAM WAS OVER.

Arriving back from the gipsy encampment, I slammed on the brakes, sending the stones flying up on my rubble-strewn drive, and I looked around at the debris of the dream. I was the owner of a house in a country that I loved, but which didn't love me, but just as a rejected lover seeks to avoid the final parting, I realised that I couldn't bring myself to let go entirely. Fudging the issue, I decided that I would continue to visit, but only rarely. For the rest of the time, I would adopt Marion's suggestion and let the house to holiday clients, and, in that context, the swimming pool would have been a good idea. Perhaps Katerina would agree to be the housekeeper, and who knows, I might even make a profit, enough at least to pay for the construction of the damned pool. With my mind made up, I was relieved when the work was finally finished, the pool filled with filtered water from the pump, the requisite chemicals added, and looking at last like the professional brochures. Perhaps I should have my photograph taken beside it, to use when I put an advertisement for clients in the paper.

"Come off it Eva," I said to myself. "You're sixty, not sixteen."

Chapter 22

Nemesis

I went to Gregory's office, to give him the final instalment for the pool, and wondered how I could break to him my plans for letting the house.

"You like the pool?" he said urgently.

"Yes, it's everything that I expected", I said.

"We must have an opening ceremony," he said. "An, how do you say? A launching, like your queen, when she pushes out a boat."

This was getting absurd. The pool had taken on the aura of the house, and now he seemed to be obsessed by both of them. I had to stop this right away.

"I was going to tell you," I said, "that I won't be living here much any more. I intend to let the house to holidaymakers for most of the year."

At first, it didn't sink in, then, he looked at me with the same puzzled expression as he had worn when I criticised him for letting his mother wash his Volvo.

"Why Eva? You can't let it to strangers. The house belongs to us here, and so do you."

I had been looking for co-operation, and it was obvious that I wasn't going to get it. Why was he so besotted? Why was he in thrall to a rocky piece of land with, let's face it, an indifferent, small house, which no one would look at twice if it wasn't in its setting of ancient Greece? However, Ancient Greece was cunning; its tentacles entwined around anyone who came within its grasp, like the serpents which wrapped round the sculpture of the apostate priest, Laecoön, and his sons. Ancient Greece had kept me at Profitis Illias, when sense had told me many times to go. Perhaps those pilgrims to Epidavros had indeed had tea on my patch of ground, and the stones were unwilling to let go of the foreigner that had dared to come and deposit herself there. Maybe Gregory was similarly affected, even though, in his case, it was instinctive and he was unaware of it. All very fanciful in the twenty-first century, but Pappa Yannis would understand; in fact, he may even be acting as surrogate for the ancient stones! I felt strangled, like that statue of Laecoön, but it made me even more determined to break the spell.

To seal the final payment on the pool, Gregory took me for coffee in the restaurant in Syntagma Square, the one with striped awnings and waiters who wore long white aprons. This was a stage upmarket from the small café round the corner, where we used to go. As I sipped the scalding black coffee, I surprised myself by reflecting that I was going to miss Gregory. I looked at his open, ingenuous face. He was still such a boy, a boy who tried to please everyone and, consequently, kept landing in trouble. Perhaps I had been too hasty in my criticism. After all, he wasn't responsible for the behaviour of the rest of the Greeks. Maybe I should have stuck to my original plan and stayed for half of each year. I could have spent more time with Magda, tracked down some obscure monuments, which hadn't yet made it to the guide books, tackled the unresponsive garden. Then, slowly, over the coffee cups, I began to think the unthinkable. Perhaps Gregory and I could get together again, we may even renew the sexual relationship; after all, he was quite good looking… !

He broke into my thoughts.

"I'm afraid I have to go," he said. "There's an international conference on land development, taking place in Athens, and I'm booked on the ten o'clock bus, because parking is impossible in Athens at this time of year. I'll be gone for three weeks, but when I get back we can talk about the house, and pool maintenance."

He leaned over and squeezed my hand, left enough money to pay for the coffee, and got up from the table. As he turned to go, he said as an afterthought,

"By the way, don't worry about the local farmers. They are an awkward lot and they'll probably complain that your pool is taking away their water. But you are within your rights in the eyes of the law and they can't do anything about it." With that, he was gone.

I sat there, stunned. All I could do was sit with my mouth open. A waiter came across to the table.

"*Tipot' allo?*" (Anything else?)

I shook my head, got up from the table, and stumbled out of the restaurant. By now, Gregory would be on the bus and, with typical insensitivity, unaware of the bombshell he had just dropped. How I found the car park by the harbour I'm not quite sure. I know that at one stage I stopped and leaned against a railing. A concerned passer-by asked me,

"*Iste kala?*" (Are you all right?)

I could only answer in English with a strangled, "Yes, yes, I'm all right."

On the way home, my mind was racing. The events of the past two years flashed through my head as if I were drowning. Now I knew why Tassos didn't come to my soirée, and why his family was so uncomfortable! From what I had seen of local farmers, Tassos included, they were not going to take this lying down. I was the owner of a house that would always be the centre of controversy. I wouldn't even be able to let it, because no agent would risk dropping a client into the middle of a vendetta. Driving round a corner, I narrowly missed a farmer on his three-wheeler bike, carrying half his family, and the near collision snapped me back into sanity. I had to end this nightmare, I had to think clearly, and there was only one satisfactory solution – I'D HAVE TO SELL THE HOUSE. How long did Gregory say he'd be away, three weeks? I had three weeks to wrap the whole thing up and get out.

Good Bye

I moved swiftly. I retrieved the deeds from the bank, went to a kleematomezitees (estate agent, remember?) in Argos and instructed him to put the house on the market. He came over to view the property, complimented me on the house and was critical of the garden. I, of course, said nothing about the pool and the water problem, but told him I needed a quick sale. Veronica was back at college, and so I sent for my eldest daughter, Jenny, to come and help me, emphasizing the need for speed. I fretted until she phoned to say that she would arrive in two day's time. I arranged to pick her up from the airport.

Meanwhile, I started to dismantle the life that had begun with such promise two years before. As I stuffed sheets and towels into plastic bags, a thought struck me. Had this all been a plot to remove me? Was Gregory's obsession with my house much more sinister, and had he engineered the whole scenario in order to take possession of my property? I dismissed the idea immediately. He would not be so devious. It was ungenerous even to think about it, and, anyway, he was strapped for cash; but it showed the state I had got into. Jenny arrived, practical and efficient, one of the new breed of powerful women, and was bowled over by the house.

"It's gorgeous," she said. "Do you have to sell it? It would make a good investment."

"Yes, I must. Too much hassle."

We worked together as a team over the next few days, until we were ready finally to load up the Mini. I reckoned that there was still time to show Jenny around a few sites. I avoided the BIG ONE because I felt that walking through the Lion gate would seriously weaken my resolve. Instead, we went to Tiryns, which had now been reopened, and then took the coastal road south of Nafplion to the town of Leonidio, where the main road peters out into secondary lanes, and the Argonic Gulf finally merges into the ocean. It was wild country, and the white houses clinging to the sides of the purple mountains looked as old as Homer. Jenny was impressed. We sat in the square in Leonidio, drinking ouzo and nibbling almonds.

"Funny," I said dreamily, "the first time I came to Greece, I met a sailor called Leopodis, lion foot, and now, when I am leaving, I'm sitting in a square in Leonidio."

"Why funny?" asked Jenny.

"Well, there aren't any lions in Greece."

We drove back through a green striped sunset. On the following day, we began packing in earnest. Although there was time to spare, I was too cowardly to face Magda. I would write to her from Wales.

The day came when we set off for Patras, and from there to Italy, then by ferry/train through France, and finally, we crossed over the channel to that island between two cold seas. The last morning, the Peloponnese outdid itself. the sky had never been so blue, the sea more clear, the scents more exotic, but as we turned the bend out of Profitis Illias, I refused to look back. I already had enough memories to serve me in the years to come. What would be my final assessment of the adventure? Only time could tell me this.

In Italy, we took the bypass at Ravenna, and I wondered again if I would ever get to see those Byzantine mosaics. Jenny did most of the driving and her body language indicated that, once more, her mother had behaved in a feckless way. First, Veronica, and now Jenny! Why didn't heaven preserve me from stroppy daughters? When I get back, I mused, I might take up with Penny, the middle one. Perhaps she would be more tolerant, a Cordelia to my King Lear.

Some weeks later, when I was in Wales, juggling with the excess pots and pans and books and bedding that I had brought back from Greece, the estate agent from Argos phoned to say that he had sold my house to a Greek from Athens.

"Fine," I thought. "He and Tassos can slog out the water rights between them – in Greek!"

I went outside, looked at the beloved, mist-covered Welsh hills and gave an enormous sigh of relief. A weight had been lifted from me, I felt free. My love for ancient Greece was undiminished, but my unsuccessful grappling with its modern version was over. I went into my stone and slate cottage and put another log on the fire.

Throughout the Spring and Summer, I wrote furiously, and finished *"Death in Greece"*, but, so far, no publisher has taken it up. The autobiography limps on; I am still stuck with the transition period from adolescence to maturity. Could it be that I have never really grown up, and I don't know anything about maturity? Perhaps I should concentrate on children's stories, or maybe I could write an account of what my daughters call "Mum's Greek adventure on the Peloponnese". Perhaps I will do just that!

Meanwhile, there has been a sting in the tail. Even though I lost money on the house, the Inland Revenue sent me a Christmas present: a bill for £450 Capital Gains Tax.

Do's and don't's when contemplating buying a house in Greece

Immediately start learning the language

The version you want is 'demotic', the everyday modern Greek, not 'katharevusa' which is strictly for academics. On the other hand, if you already have grammar/public school grounding in Ancient Greek, it will help you to stumble through (viz. The boys of the Special Operations Executive during the Second World War). According to the Greek Embassy there are over 200 courses for studying Greek in the UK. I used the City Lit. in Holborn, but if you are not interested in attending classes, there is a BBC TV series called Talk Greek which is transmitted regularly on the BBC Learning Zone.

Decide on an area

Sea-view properties are more expensive than inland. Make no decisions after one heavenly trip, but visit several times, especially during the winter months.

Choose an agent

...preferably a local English-speaking one. He will deal with the bureaucracy, arrange a notary to deal with the money side, and he will also check on any bylaws relating to the property you select.

Having found a place, sleep on it, not once, but twice. Consider access: distance from airport, motorways, railways, nearest main town, etc.

Finally...

If you are a lone woman, test the water. Go to your nearest café and find out (your Greek should be adequate by now) a) is your local area/town/village dominated by religious bigots and b) what is the attitude of the men to foreign women.

References

Internet: www.property-abroad.com

Buying a House in Greece, Joanna Styles (Survival Books), £11.95

Sunday Times Guide to Buying a Property in Greece, Mary Dublin, £12.99

Enquiries: The Education Officer, Embassy of Greece, 1A Holland Park, London 2113TP